the easy fruit garden

the easy fruit garden

Clare Matthews

NEW HOLLAND

Published in 2012 by New Holland Publishers (UK) Ltd
London • Cape Town • Sydney • Auckland

www.newhollandpublishers.com

Garfield House, 86–88 Edgware Road, London W2 2EA,
United Kingdom

80 McKenzie Street, Cape Town 8001, South Africa

Unit 1, 66 Gibbes Street, Chatswood, NSW 2067, Australia

218 Lake Road, Northcote, Auckland, New Zealand

A catalogue record for this book is available from the British Library.

ISBN 978 1 78009 154 9

Commissioning editor: Emma Pattison
Designer: Geoff Borin
Special photography: Clive Nichols
Production controller: Laurence Poos

10 9 8 7 6 5 4 3 2 1

Reproduction by Modern Age Repro House Ltd, Hong Kong
Printed and bound in China by C&C Offset Printing Co., Ltd

contents

introduction

I have a passion for growing my own food. I am unashamedly evangelical about how wonderful and easy the 'grow your own' experience can be if kept simple and expectations reasonable. I firmly believe that if you spend any time at all tending your garden you could be growing at least a couple of types of fruit, as most fruiting plants are no more challenging to grow than run-of-the mill shrubs.

I first grew fruit in my vegetable patch and it worked really well. The fruiting plants were a permanent, undemanding part of the garden that produced hefty harvests of succulent berries. When I moved house and set about planning a new productive garden, I realized I could grow a great deal more fruit without much more work so long as I used all the tricks I had learned from my first veg plot.

Most fruiting plants are long-lived and the maintenance is minimal. I liked the idea of picking more of my own organically-grown fruit. It is a healthy option enjoyed by the whole family in puddings, preserves and, best of all, straight from the plant.

My fruit garden has proved incredibly easy to manage, though its construction stretched over a number of months as I gradually filled beds, planted and added my finishing touches. This initial flurry of effort definitely paid off. It is a marvellous place to spend time and now I can look forward to literally years and years of fabulous fruit.

This book concentrates on presenting just what you really need to know about growing your own fruit, and the easiest ways to get a bountiful harvest. Challenging, time consuming horticultural techniques are ignored in favour of describing just the bare essentials, sensible short cuts and simplest routes to tasty home grown fruit.

My hope is to give everyone enough confidence to embark upon growing at least some fruit and experience the very real delight of growing your own. Good luck!

Clare Matthews

why grow your own fruit?

Home-grown fruit is delicious, nutritious and inexpensive to produce. It's no more difficult to grow than many ornamental plants, and a great deal easier than others. Some fruits really cannot be bought in anything like the superb condition you can experience if you grow them yourselves. 'Home-grown taste' is a phase often bandied about, but it is just as true of fruit as it is of veg. There is an intensity and freshness to the taste of fruit you have grown yourself that is really very special. (I have often wondered if the satisfaction of knowing you produced the crop isn't flavour enhancing.) You know how it has been grown. It will be free of pesticides, herbicides and chemical fertilizers, unless you choose to use them and then you will know they have been applied responsibly. Dedicated fruit gardens can be beautiful if you chose to grow your fruit that way, or productive trees and bushes can successfully be part of the planting in a family garden. Even if you only have a balcony or small outdoor space, you can still grow your own fruit in pots.

Children find growing fruit even more alluring than growing veg, often grazing their way through what would be punnets full of vitamin packed raspberries, blueberries and strawberries as they walk by the plants. Fruits that are expensive to buy are a breeze to grow. The abundance can be staggering and everyone can indulge themselves.

the ground rules

Grow what you enjoy eating – there is an amazing array of fruits available. There are new or rediscovered fruits that often become the latest 'thing' to grow. I have tried many but none have matched up to my old favourites.

Choose plants that are suited to your environment and circumstances. Doing battle with nature is a relentless, exhausting task, so make canny choices in what you grow. For example, if you suffer from late frosts, avoid varieties with blossom that might be damaged. Likewise if you live in cold area, there is no point devoting space and time to trying to grow melons or passion fruit outside. If you are unlikely to get around to pruning, don't try to grow fan-trained and espalier trees.

Select vigorous cultivars that have good resistance to pests and diseases. There are cultivars that just require more pampering than others to give their best, and are likely to be a martyr to every kind of pest and disease going. Not only is this time consuming to deal with, it will limit the harvest and is generally irksome

Right *Growing your own fruit is wonderfully rewarding, and the bushes or trees can be decorative, too.*

and disappointing. Much easier to grow the toughies – the stalwarts that will grow well, have some disease resistance and will shrug off pests yet still produce a fantastic harvest of delicious fruit.

Plant well. With any luck most fruit bushes will be delivering up their bounty for at least 10 years, and fruit and nut trees for tens and even hundreds of years, so it is definitely worthwhile ensuring they are planted into the best soil you can provide, in the right way and in the right place.

Take it slowly. Though growing fruit is far less time consuming than veg, it is still best to plan things at a manageable pace. If growing fruit is a new venture there is no problem in having big dreams if you take things in manageable chunks. Sitting with a nursery catalogue in summer and enthusiastically ordering several of everything will leave you with hours of work to build and prepare beds, if you are starting from scratch, before the parcels of bareroot plants start arriving in autumn. Planning will mean you start with a good idea of just how much time and resources you have to invest.

Do what is essential to get a crop. There are many wonderful, beautiful and interesting things you can do in the fruit garden – train and bend trees into intricate patterns, graft several cultivars of fruit onto one root stock, or grow trees from seed. They are not theoretically beyond anyone willing to take the trouble, but all take patience, skill and a significant chunk of time are not worthwhile for the time-poor gardener who just wants the joy of eating good fruit straight from the garden.

the bare essentials

- Water young plants in dry weather until they are well established.
- Feed all bushes, plants, canes and young trees with an all-purpose, organic fertilizer in early spring.
- Apply a mulch of good garden compost or well-rotted farmyard manure around all bushes, canes and young trees in early spring.
- Prune if essential.
- Use paper mulches, grass clippings, companion plants or other organic mulch to keep soil covered and limit weeds.
- Use a seaweed liquid feed as a foliar spray if a plant looks as if it needs a bit of a boost, or is weakened by pests or disease.

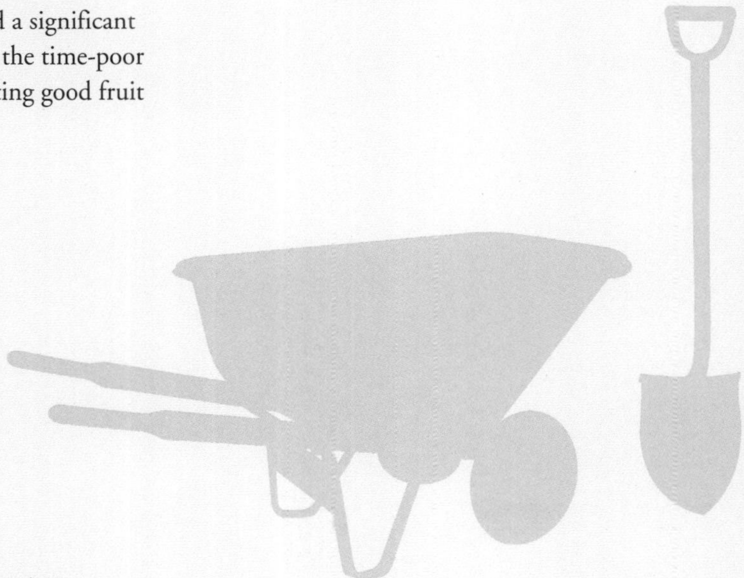

Left *This greenhouse is dedicated to growing melons and watermelons.*

planning and design

Whatever size your garden and however little time you have, there is a way you can grow fruit. If you have plenty of space, you could set out an area dedicated to growing fruit. But even a small corner can yield plenty of tasty fruit if the type of fruit is chosen wisely. In tiny plots or paved yards many fruit bushes will thrive in pots, straw bales or grow bags.

Above *For those who are short of space, container growing can generate some reasonable harvests.*

planning

how and what to grow

Fruit bushes can be productive for around 10 years, possibly 15. Fruit trees may be productive for a hundred years or more, and they have the potential to provide plenty of delicious food, bursting with health-promoting vitamins and chemicals, so it is just good sense to plan what to grow and where to grow it carefully. Thought and effort put in at the planning stage will definitely make life easier as plants will be well matched to your needs, and the space in which you choose to grow them. These are the two key areas to look at: what to grow and where to grow it. The two are obviously inextricably linked, but it makes sense to start with what to grow, purely because there is no point whatsoever in growing fruit you don't want to eat (unless it is to attract wildlife into your patch, but that is a for a different book).

Start with a wishlist of what you would like to grow, things you and you family love to eat most, or fruit you would like to make preserves with. Next, look at the space you have available. Are you planning a large fruit garden, pots on the terrace or balcony, or simply covering a stretch of wall? Wandering around an established garden with fresh eyes can often reveal opportunities as yet unthought of.

At this stage it will probably help to make a list or draw out a plan of the areas you have available for planting. A scale plan is best if you are planning a large formal fruit garden, while a quick sketch of the garden with potential locations might suffice for those slotting fruit into existing beds. Now start assigning your wishlist plants to the space you have available.

considerations

When planning your fruit garden it is worth considering the following:

• The height and spread of the plant, and the spacing if you intend to plant in rows.

• Each plant's preferred growing conditions.

• The likely annual yield once the plants are established. There is little point planting 10 gooseberry bushes, for example, which might yield a whopping 40 kg (88 lb) of fruit and take up 12 m (40 ft) of growing space, when all you want is enough gooseberries for a few pies!

• How long you will wait for a harvest. Growing fruit is fun and, although there is something to be said for the intense satisfaction of savouring the fruit from a tree you have nurtured for, say, five years, getting at least some rewards the first year of cultivation is enormously encouraging and exciting. It may be best to have some plants which provide almost instant gratification amongst the longer-term propositions.

• The amount of work required to grow each plant and the level of care each plant requires. There is no point filling your space with demanding prima donnas, with blossom that needs protecting from frost, who require an exacting pruning regime to fruit well and weekly feeding, if you know you don't have the time to devote to them.

• Look at the scale of the whole project you have in mind. Can you easily manage that number of plants? In many ways the first year of the fruit tree or bush is the most demanding. The planting areas need preparing, planting needs to be done and the plants require regular watering while they establish. Planting a truck load of plants in one hit may seem like a good idea, but it may pay to split the planting over two years so the plants get reasonable care and growing your own fruit remains enjoyable rather than a chore. Once the first year is over the care required is minimal.

Below *When planning your garden do not forget vital, practical elements such as the compost bin.*

which fruits to grow where

Below are some lists you may find useful when planning how and what to grow. This information is also given in the detailed directory entries for each fruit on pages 54–140, but it is here as well to make planning easy.

the easiest fruits

- Autumn raspberries
- Summer fruiting raspberries
- Alpine strawberries
- Japanese wine berries
- Rhubarb (not a fruit, but a 'culinary fruit')
- Blackberries
- Gooseberries
- Apples
- Hazels
- Walnuts

the most difficult fruits

- Peaches
- Almonds
- Fan trained stone fruit
- Restrictively trained fruit trees

Above left *These succulent 'Autumn Bliss' raspberries are amongst the easiest and tastiest fruits you can grow. Add a layer of mulch in early spring and cut the whole plant to the ground in winter.*

Left *To enjoy plenty of peaches like this from your garden, conditions will have to be just right and your pruning spot on.*

Right *Cleverly trained fruit trees are delightful but the work, knowledge and foresight required to create these magnificent shapes and then maintain them is probably best left to the enthusiast and professional, not the relaxed time-poor gardener.*

fruit to grow up sunny walls and fences

- Kiwi
- Summer raspberries
- Blackberries (and their hybrids)
- Japanese wineberries
- Red currants, grown as cordons
- Figs
- Fan-trained peaches, apricots and nectarines
- Gooseberries grown as cordons
- Passion fruit
- Grapes

fruit for shady walls

- Morello cherry
- Blackberries
- Japanese wine berries

most likely to fruit in areas with late frost

- Damsons
- Sour/morello cherries
- Plum 'Czar' and 'Marjories seedling'
- Late flowering blackcurrants, 'Ben Tirran' is just about the latest of all.
- Apples 'Egremont Russet', Discovery, Laxton's Superb, Spartan
- Pear 'Invincible'

ornamental fruit

- Kiwi
- Japanese wine berries
- Fig
- Passion fruit
- Standard blackcurrant
- Standard redcurrant
- Standard gooseberry
- Some blueberries
- Trained fruit trees

Above left *The young leaves of the kiwi are like delicate stained glass when illuminated by the sun. The vine is a strong grower and will quickly cover a wall if given a trellis or wires to spiral around.*

Left *Blackberries will do fairly well in partial shade but the fruit will lack the sweetness it gains from ripening in the sun.*

fruit for quick results

Soft fruits including:

- Strawberries
- Raspberries
- Blackberries
- Blueberries
- All the currants

fruit for containers

- All fruit trees described as patio trees or on a dwarfing rootstock
- All minaret and ballerina fruit trees
- Black currants
- Figs
- Blueberries
- Strawberries
- Redcurrants
- Gooseberries
- Grapes
- Cape gooseberry
- Melon

not recommended for containers

Some of these may prosper in a pot for a year or two but long-term they will not prosper, yield will be low and unworthy of the effort of caring for them.

- Blackberries
- Raspberries
- Loganberries
- Japanese wineberries
- Kiwi

Above right *These sour cherries are more likely to fruit in areas with late frosts than the sweet cultivars.*

Right *The unusually shaped leaves of this aptly named fig 'Ice Crystal' make it particularly ornamental. The tree produces small, tasty fruits.*

design

where to position the fruit garden

If you have the space then dedicating an area, however small, to growing fruit is a real luxury. The area can have much the same feel as the veg plot – it can be formal in design, decorative or more workaday. There is no one solution to the best garden for you, but ensure it has a design that pleases you, fits the space and will accommodate the fruit you want to grow. Fruit gardens sit well next to the veg patch, united by their practical intent and requirements. Both benefit from a warm sheltered spot, both should allow easy access to the plants being grown, and both need ready access to the compost heap, leafmould bins and water butt.

You might even decide to dispense with the freeloading shrubs and perennials and opt for plants that are no harder to care for but that really earn their keep, turning your whole outdoor space into a fruit lover's paradise. The fruit garden can look splendid, whether large or small. Designing the area carefully, adding decorative touches, stylish furniture and colourful companion planting will make the garden a special place to spend time. In my fruit garden I have three different places to sit. Each catches the sun at a different time of day and it is one of my favourite spots to spend a few quiet moments with a cup of tea.

location

For the best fruit possible for the least effort you need to select the most appropriate area in your garden, or make a few changes to improve what space you have available. The ideal site will be warm, sunny and sheltered, with a good, fertile, reasonably deep, well-drained, moisture-retentive soil. Sun and light ripen fruit, making it sweet and delicious. At a pinch, sunshine for about half the day in the summer will suffice for most fruits, except for the real sun lovers – figs, apricots, peaches and grapes. The only exception would be in very hot countries where some shade from the sun in the hottest part of the day would be essential. Fruit blossom and fruits are easily damaged by extreme weather, high winds, frost and driving rain. High winds will also disrupt the activities of pollinating insects, which are vital to a good crop.

A wind break can be added to protect an area. It might form part of the garden's design, dividing it from other parts of the garden, and it can, of course, be decorative. It is tempting to imagine that a solid fence or thick evergreen hedge might do the best job at protecting fruit from the wind, but in reality the force of the wind is diverted upwards by solid structures and tumbles over the top of them causing turbulence amongst the plants you are trying to protect. Better to think about filtering the wind, breaking it up and slowing it down through open fences, stout trellis or open hedges, such as beech.

If you can, avoid growing your fruit in a frost pocket. This means an area which is colder for longer than the surrounding garden because the cold air is trapped in the area, making it more likely to suffer from frosts. It can be simple to alleviate problems – perhaps the cold air is being trapped by garden features such as solid fences or hedges, which can be opened up slightly near ground level to allow the cold air to seep away. If a frosty spot is the only possible choice then choose late flowering, robust cultivars of the most frost-tolerant fruits and, if possible, cover vulnerable blossom with horticultural fleece to give the best chance of success.

Right *This is my fruit garden – a stretch of flat, sunny lawn converted into something far more satisfying and productive.*

the fruit garden design

Before you begin to think about design, check you have all of the following information: a location, an idea of what fruit you would most like to pick from your own patch, how many bushes of each you might need to grow, and how much space they will require to flourish. You can then draw all of this information together and plan how to lay out your planting areas. Having a series of beds, possibly raised, bounded by paths will undoubtedly produce a garden that is easier to maintain than an open allotment-style garden. In the open garden there is a lot of space that is not productive to maintain. Using conveniently sized beds you can concentrate your efforts on the areas that matter. It is also a simple matter to protect the fruit within a bed from birds or frost with canes and mesh or fleece. You might choose to construct raised beds to escape difficult soil conditions, or simply cut beds into an area of turf.

the plan

Even the smallest of spaces benefit from being planned on paper. A rough sketch will do, with the basic dimensions of your proposed fruit area. In fact, it is often the smallest spaces that benefit most from a few moments trying different arrangements of paths and beds on paper. Beds should be just short of twice the length of your arm at most so plants can easily be tended without trampling the soil. The length is best limited too, otherwise walking around beds to get to others becomes tiresome. Note down what you intend to plant in each bed and how many plants will be needed. Traditional space allowances are based on the rows of the open, allotment-style garden. In a garden with beds, bushes can be arranged in staggered double rows to get the most out of the space, so plants are planted in blocks. But remember you will need to get to the fruit.

Keep things simple and easy to maintain. Make the garden no bigger than you need and keep all personal flourishes and flights of fancy maintenance-free. In other words, better to go for sensibly-sized square and rectangular beds than an intricate pattern of box edged dolls house sized beds. Add character and interest with ornaments, objet trouvé, furniture and sculpture.

Left *Basic carpentry skills are all that is required to make these simple raised beds. Constructed from 25 x 4 cm (10 x 1½ in) boards and 10 x 10 cm (4 x 4 in) corner posts cut to length by a timber yard and assembled using long wood screws to attach the planks to the posts.*

raised beds

Building some form of raised bed has the benefit of escaping poor or problem soil. The addition of the raised framework allows an excellent growing medium to be built up in the beds. Soil that drains too freely and lacks fertility is simple to deal with by adding 30 cm (12 in) to 50 cm (18 in) deep beds crammed with beefed-up soil. Poor drainage is slightly trickier to escape and depends on the scale of the problem. Soil that is just a little sticky will probably only require the same sort of treatment as light soil. If water often pools on the surface of the soil then it may be necessary to improve the drainage before constructing very deep raised beds.

If the soil under the raised beds is clean and weed free, a mix of about 50/50 good quality topsoil and garden compost, or well rotted manure, can be used to fill the beds. Remember when you are filling the beds that the soil level will drop a little as the contents consolidate, so fill them generously. Any drop in level simply makes room for mulch later. There is an alternative way to fill raised beds, by building up deep bed mulch (see pages 34–35).

paths

Paths in your fruit garden should provide easy access to the fruit growing in the beds, making getting at the ripe fruit an easy matter. If you are lucky enough not to be short of space then make all of the paths passable with a wheel barrow, remembering that plants will spill from the beds. If space is tight, plan some narrower paths but ensure that at least some part of each planting area is bounded by a path fit for the wheelbarrow – it makes lugging mulch around the garden so much easier.

The ideal path for the easy fruit garden is durable, effortlessly attractive, maintenance free and usable in all weathers. Paving stones, brick and gravel all make excellent, long lasting paths. Laying any kind of paving requires an investment of both time and money and some skill, and gravel is the easier, almost instant, option. A heavy duty weed suppressing membrane can be pinned securely over the network of paths, and a 5–7.5 cm (2–3 in) layer of gravel added on top. If you have raised beds, the membrane can be tucked securely under the bottom edges of the beds to stop weeds finding a way through. If you are using low beds then a low timber edge will be needed to delineate the path and retain the gravel. Grass paths can look fantastic if they are well maintained and the ground is well drained, and if you are building your fruit patch on an area of lawn they are already there – the quickest and easiest option. Some people opt for bark chip paths, but for me this is the worst surface possible. The chips scatter across the garden when they are dry; when wet they clog together, stick to boots and wheelbarrow wheels, and eventually rot down to a brown sludge.

Above left *Wonderfully weathered slabs of timber, surrounded by gravel, make a practical and characterful path that is simple to construct.*

Above right *A significant amount of time and expense has gone into constructing this rather grand path. Brick, stone and gravel combine to great effect.*

Right *There are a myriad of materials that can be combined to make a sensible path. Here gravel, interspersed with slabs of timber, make a simple but striking path.*

fruit trees

Patio, minaret or ballerina fruit trees might be planted within the beds. Used to add height and contribute to the visual appeal of the garden, it would be more usual to plant larger trees outside the beds. They can be used as focal points or to divide the space. The most important point to remember when planting a tree is how much they will grow. Most of us plant single trees, and they always look rather skinny and forlorn when newly planted, barely occupying any space and casting only a match stick's shadow. Move on a few years and that same tree should have thickened up and be sporting a healthy canopy, so imagine how this larger tree will sit in your design. Will it be casting shade on a real sun-lover, stopping light from reaching house windows or causing a nuisance to a neighbour?

Below *'President' plum trees on a very dwarfing root stock, under-planted with lavender 'Hidcote', line the central path of my fruit garden.*

supports

Growing fruit that can be trained neatly against a vertical support is a real space saving option, as the plants provide a good harvest but occupy very little growing space. Cane fruits, kiwi and passion fruit all need some form of support. This can be purely practical, taking advantage of existing structures by stretching along an existing wall, fence or even the side of a shed. Or the supports can be more decorative, providing the opportunity to add height to the garden, and build screens and divides to shape the garden's structure.

posts and wires

If attaching wires to an existing fence, wall or shed is not an option, a series of freestanding posts can be erected and strung with wires. In my garden the posts are part of the structure of the raised beds. This means the posts are not actually set in the ground, which makes construction much easier. There is no limit to how posts and wires might be configured: short individual panels or a long run to form a boundary, a zig-zagged screen or even a u-shaped arbour. The principles and construction are incredibly simple but, because it is so flexible, it offers plenty of opportunities to be creative. Generally the post should be about 2–2.25 m (6–7 ft) tall with horizontal wires about 30–50 cm (12–18 in) apart. This set-up will suit all kinds of fruit.

Once the posts are erected mark the positions for the wire supports on the posts carefully. Measuring these accurately is important or else your wires may not be perfectly vertical. Screw the vine eyes into position – if your posts are soft wood it should be easy enough to do this by hand. Finally add the 'wire'. This is not actually a metal wire but a tough plastic. This has the advantage that it can be used with neat plastic tensioning devices that grip the wire and enable you

Above right *With this simple system, a black plastic cord is held taut by a nifty, easy-to-use tensioning device.*

Right *In the finished bed raspberries, sweet peas and cordon red currants are all being ably supported.*

to pull the wire perfectly taut, and does not allow it to slip back so getting neat, ramrod straight wires, rather than sad washing lines. It is amazingly simple and much easier than wire, which can easily become kinked and bent.

arches, obelisks, pergolas and arbours

For something more showy, raspberries and blackberries can be trained up large ornate obelisks, bent to clothe arches, or even spiralled up a single, free-standing post. For very confined growing conditions choose less vigorous cultivars, such as the blackberry 'Waldo', to avoid tying them in becoming a battle and the plant literally swamping the structure. If you have a sheltered pergola to clothe however, a vigorous grape vine or passion fruit would be an excellent choice.

Above *Set at the side of the fruit garden, orientated to catch the sun in the morning and planted with robust grape vines, this straightforward structure will make a sheltered seating area once the vines become established. To a u-shaped raised bed with the same simple construction as the others in the garden, a simple trellis work of lengths roofing battens has been added. The same structure could be furnished with wires rather than battens for a similar effect*

fruit cages

Defending soft fruit against attack from birds is one task that really cannot be overlooked. While some fruits are more vulnerable than others, blueberries, red currants and sweet cherries tend to be favoured, while sour cherries and blackcurrants are often left until last, and all need protection before they ripen. It is perfectly possible to do this by moving home-spun constructions of netting or chick wire supported on canes around the garden as different fruits become vulnerable. The alternative is to provide your fruit garden with a fruit cage. This is a permanent framework of vertical and horizontal metal poles, high enough to walk around in with ease, which span the whole soft fruit growing area. Before fruit ripens the framework is covered in netting which is carefully secured to the framework and the ground. This need not be a costly construction; basic kits are available from DIY stores and garden centres. The nets should be removed in the winter to allow the birds in to clear away pests and any remaining fruit.

Above *In the first bed a heavy crop of 'Sunshine Blue' blueberries is being ably protected by a chickwire tent.*

Below *This is the most enchanting fruit cage – a Victorian aviary which now, rather ironically, is used to keep the birds out rather than pen them in.*

Above *This elegantly curved bench is a gentle full stop at the end of the vista through the centre of my productive garden, before the garden merges with the countryside beyond. Its stylish contours make it immensely comfortable.*

looking good

Growing your own fruit can be a simple matter of planting a few strawberries in a flower pot on the terrace, or as adventurous as turning your whole plot over to fruiting plants. Wherever your fruit growing project falls between these two extremes, making it look good as well as productive will make the whole project far more rewarding. Keeping one eye on making the garden attractive and a comfortable place to spend time makes working outside more of a pleasure, making it more likely that the bits and pieces of maintenance get done.

The layout of the garden will go a long way to ensuring its good looks, what is often referred to as giving a garden 'good bones'. If the pattern of beds looks tidy, the garden will look good even if the contents of the beds are less than orderly. Adding personal touches will really bring the garden to life. Sculptures, objet trouvé or a colourful well-placed bench will all make your patch special. Even the labels you choose (it is best to label – two years time and you might not be able to bring to mind the exact cultivar you planted) can be decorative, in chunky slate, shining copper or oversized homemade stained wooden batten. All look good and enhance the garden and gardening.

Above right *The arrangement of beds does not have to be complicated to look good. The arrangement of these chunky beds could not be simpler, but the garden looks attractive and, most importantly, it is easy to maintain.*

Right *Although it is yet to be festooned with vines and dripping with grapes, this home-spun arbour is already a superb place to sit, relax and catch the morning sun.*

Far right *At the heart of the garden is a seemingly gravity-defying sculpture by Paul Margetts, encircled by a planting of nectar-rich perennials. An amazing feat of balance and artistry, the elements of the sculpture move independently of each other in just the slightest breeze to make ever changing forms.*

preparation

preparing the soil

Good soil preparation before planting can be hard work, but giving plants the best growing conditions possible will give the best chance of a sturdy, healthy plant and generous crop of perfect fruit. If you are setting out new fruit beds, you have the chance to create a great growing medium which will really set up your fruit bushes and canes wonderfully.

The more traditional way to prepare a plot would be some good old fashioned digging, or even the far more tortuous double-digging. However, I favour the no-dig method to manage my garden and deep bed mulching to prepare planting areas. Not only is it easier, it works, and arguably it produces a much healthier soil. The soil is in essence a complex habitat for millions of microorganisms vital to soil fertility. Digging wrecks the soil structure and disturbs the balance of these soil dwelling organisms, makes soil more likely to dry out and leaves a bare, broken soil surface perfect for colonisation by weeds. The improvement that the digging gardener claims to get from her labours, I encourage the worms and soil micro fauna to do for me.

No-dig gardening relies on improving soil fertility and soil structure by adding piles of organic matter which is broken down and pulled into the soil by worms. This is done once a year – a layer of about 7.5 cm (3 in) of good garden compost, or well-rotted farmyard manure, is spread over the soil around young fruit trees or over entire fruit beds. It can usefully be done anytime from mid autumn until early spring, so long as the soil is not waterlogged or frozen. I normally opt for early spring, so the nutrients will not have been leached away in the winter and will be ready for the plants in that growing season. This annual mulch is one of the very few essential tasks in the easy fruit garden. Having said this, once your fruit plants are established skipping a year would not be a disaster. You would, however, lose the weed suppressing and moisture retentive benefits the mulch delivers.

miraculous deep bed mulch

If the soil where you plan to grow your fruit is weedy, turf or just populated by small plants, then you have the opportunity to use my favourite planting area preparation. It is inexpensive, easy, low skilled and still produces a beautifully fertile growing medium. It is known by various names, including the rather marvellous 'lasagne gardening', because materials are built up in layers. Essentially the technique involves burying the existing and unwanted plants under a layer of thick card or a hefty slab of newspaper, layers of organic matter and perhaps some top soil. This is undoubtedly easier and more controllable when done within the confines of a raised bed, but heaping up the materials to form a fertile pillow-shaped bed will work – it is just a little untidy and uncontrollable. The layered materials can slip and spread without a framework to hold them together. The layers can be built up over a number of months as material becomes available, so long as the initial layers are really holding down the cardboard or paper securely, or piled-up in just one day. Unlike clearing the soil this process feels a great deal more positive and will almost certainly leave you with a much better growing medium.

The initial cardboard or paper layer ensures the weeds are thoroughly smothered and deprived of light, and this layer gradually rots away. The growth can be trodden down, or cut back with a strimmer, to ensure the card can be put in place easily. Don't be tempted to try this method without this bottom layer, as organic material alone is unlikely to do the trick. Annual weeds are killed off easily, their seeds are buried too deep to succeed and although some really tough perennial weeds might be expected to survive and grow through, in my experience it seldom happens and those that do are easily despatched.

A whole host of organic materials can be used to build up the layers, any which might harbour weed seeds. Hay, for example, should be put below the cardboard layer. The layers should be no thicker than 15 cm (6 in) and, as with compost, lush green material such as grass clippings should be followed by coarser, drier brown material such as torn up newspaper or fallen leaves.

materials to use in deep bed mulching

- Well-rotted manure
- Straw
- Hay
- Coffee grounds
- Shredded newspaper
- Garden compost
- Wood ash (ensure no plastics were burned in the fire)
- Seaweed
- Kitchen waste (no cooked food or meat)
- Tops of weeds such as nettles (not in flower or setting seed)
- Grass cuttings
- Leafmould
- Fallen leaves (but only in thin layers as they can form a slow rotting mat)
- Spent potting compost
- Mushroom compost
- Rotted sawdust
- Top soil (I tend to include at least two layers)

If you are short of raw material, riding stables are usually only too happy to be rid of manure and farmers will normally deliver a trailer load. Beg grass clippings and fallen leaves from neighbours, stock pile kitchen waste and save ash from fires and bonfires, and get friends to do the same. One important factor to consider when building up a stock of material to use is to ensure none are harbouring weed seeds or roots. These may spring into life, spoiling all your hard work. Garden compost can harbour seeds and sections of root if it has been made indiscriminately.

Above *Vegetable peelings are excellent for use in deep bed mulching, and are free, too! Keep a bucket handy in your kitchen to collect the peelings.*

deep mulch raised bed

1 Line the bed or cover the area with cardboard. Unprinted, unglazed, plain corrugated card is best, and flattened out heavy-duty boxes are ideal. Allow a good overlap where pieces of card meet and lap the card up the sides of the wooden beds, pushing the card well into the corner where the bed edge joins the ground. If you use newspaper use it lavishly as you don't want this barrier to breakdown too quickly.

2 Add the first layer of material. At most the layer should be 10–15 cm (4–6 in) thick. Gently firm the layers down as you go, but there's no need to trample it down.

3 Next add a further layer just a few centimetres thick, remembering to alternate materials – lush and green should be followed by dry and brown. Well-rotted manure and top soil are great anywhere in the mix.

4 Finish with a layer of top soil and ideally leave the bed to mature for a month or two before planting. If you need to plant bareroot plants immediately and the materials you have used are very fresh, create small planting pockets of topsoil.

clearing the soil the hard way

To prepare the soil all the weeds must be removed. If you are in a hurry and don't want to use a deep bed mulch, the only solution is to dig them out, taking care to get all the roots out (one of the few essential occasions when this disturbance is necessary). You don't have to dig over the whole area in the traditional way, just do what is necessary to remove the weeds or plants. This does have to be done quite carefully, with as much of the roots extracted as possible. Many weeds are real survivors and will regrow from a tiny section of root. In fact, breaking the weed roots up as you try to remove them can help weeds such as bindweed multiply.

If you have the time and the patience then weeds can be killed by smothering them with a heavy duty weed suppressing membrane, layers of cardboard or thick black plastic held firmly in place. This denies the weeds light and will eventually kill them. It requires little effort but plenty of patience and forward planning as sadly as the weeds might require several months or up to a year before they are completely dead. It also means that you will be spending months looking at a fairly unattractive area. In areas that have plenty of hot sunshine the weeds can be despatched more quickly by using a covering of black polythene and relying on the heat of the sun to warm the polythene and the plants under it to such an extent that they will perish.

Once the soil is weed-free, pile on a good layer of garden compost or well-rotted manure. The perfect preparation guide would demand this was done several months in advance of planting to allow the almost magical transformation of the mulch into a brown crumbly soil. However, if you only get around to piling the mulch on just before planting, it will do. Just scrape the mulch back and plant, mixing a little mulch into the soil you put around the plant, and then draw it back up around the plant to within a couple of centimetres of its stem.

Above *Sometimes there is no way to avoid removing weeds by hand. Take care to remove all of the root or you will be doing it again in a few weeks time.*

Left *Once the soil is clear of weeds, a good layer of garden compost or well-rotted manure can be spread on its surface.*

where to grow fruit

container growing

If you have limited garden space or are planning to grow your fruit in a paved yard or on a balcony, then growing fruit in containers is very straightforward. A surprising number of types of fruit will flourish and produce a worthwhile crop in pots. The only down side is growing plants in any kind of container requires good care routine as the plants are dependent on the gardener. The tasks are not difficult but cannot be neglected as regular watering and feeding are needed to keep them not just productive but alive. If you have the option of growing your fruit directly in the ground, take it, as it is undoubtedly much easier.

grow bags and straw bales

The grow bag is an instant, off-the-shelf container and compost in one. They are easy but not the prettiest things to have sat on the terrace or balcony. Trays and troughs to disguise them are available, but then this is much the same as filling a pot with good compost. The size and contents of bags vary. Organic versions are available and many contain extra nutrients or materials to stop the compost drying out too quickly. The only fruit suited to grow bag cultivation are strawberries and melons, and bags specifically designed for strawberries are available. In both cases go for the larger bags, as they allow the plants to develop a good root system and will not dry out so quickly. Rather than using the bags flat, stand them on end – a little squashing and remoulding before they are opened should get them standing safely. Plant one melon plant in the top of the bag, or cut small slots around the bag and slot strawberry plants in, mimicking the traditional strawberry pot. Grow bags need plenty of water and the plants will need regular liquid feeds after the first few weeks.

With its pleasing rustic good looks the straw bale is an appealing alternative to growing fruit in pots or grow bags. The straw provides an efficient, inexpensive growing medium, which is easy to manage. As the straw bale decomposes, nutrients are made available to the plant and heat is released promoting growth – a clear advantage over grow bags. Though the bales decomposition is part of the process a good bale should last a couple of years, then it can be added to the compost heap or used as mulch. Don't be tempted to use a hay bale. It is possible but they will break down quickly and usually contain a great number of grass and weed seeds.

Right *Strawberry plants do well in the very confined space of a hanging baskets, so long as they are hung in a sheltered spot and kept well fed and watered.*

Below *Melons grown in a large container, provided with an obelisk to scale, are both decorative and fruitful.*

straw bale growing

1 Put your straw bale into position with the string running across the top and onto the ground. This means water will seep slowly through the bale rather than rushing through. Before you plant your bale, prepare it by watering well for four or five days so that the first surge of heat produced by its decomposition passes before planting, as the temperature rise may be high enough to damage the plants. Include an organic liquid feed.

2 Arrange your plants. They can be planted in the top and sides of the bale. If the bale is not tightly-packed it may be possible to simply form a hole for each plant by pulling the straw apart. In a good, tightly-packed bale use a bread or carving knife to create a hole. Take care not to cut the string.

3 Once you have formed the planting holes, add a good handful of multi-purpose compost to each. Press the compost down to leave room for the plant's root ball.

straw bale growing

4 Gently push the root balls of the plants into the straw. Here I have used a grafted melon 'Sweet heart', four strawberry plants and some trailing nasturtiums.

5 Water the bale regularly to keep the straw damp and feed with a liquid feed once every couple of weeks. Using a seep hose draped around the plants in the top of the bale is very effective for irrigating straw bales, especially if you have a run of bales

6 After a couple of seasons add the straw to the compost heap or use as mulch on the fruit garden. It will still be a hefty mulch, great for protecting bare soil around fruit bushes over the winter.

potted fruit

Pots planted with fruiting plants can be every bit as decorative as growing floriferous annuals, a great deal more interesting and your care is rewarded with a tasty harvest. Choose a decorative container and select your fruiting plants carefully. Add some flowering companion plants and you can successfully dress-up a terrace. Some plants will prove more fruitful than others, producing a very worthwhile crop. Realistically, however, harvests are obviously more restricted than plants in open ground. Most plants will need a sheltered sunny spot. One of the bonuses of container growing is that plants can be moved around to take advantage of the weather, exploiting the warm microclimates formed by paving and walls to give good growth in the summer and protect plants from frosts in the winter. It is also easy to net container grown fruit to prevent birds from feasting on your crop before you can. You also have control over the soil your fruit is growing in; container growing is an obvious solution when growing acid-loving plants such as blueberries and cranberries.

The downside of container growing is that the plants are almost completely dependent on you, the gardener, for everything they need except some irrigation from rainfall, which cannot be relied upon. Plants will need regular watering and feeding if they are to produce a good crop. In warm weather pots may need watering twice a day. Using generously sized pots can help as small pots dry out more quickly, thoigh avoid over-potting. The other option is to install a simple irrigation system. This takes all the drudgery out of watering, and with a timer you don't even have to remember to turn it on. A simple system can be put together with components from garden centres. (See page 192 for more on watering.) Aim to keep the compost damp, as too much or too little water can cause the young fruit to drop.

Some of the best, most striking subjects for container growing are fruit trees on dwarfing rootstocks, either as small trees or as cordons or ballerina trees. Even a small balcony could accommodate a potted orchard, replete with all kinds of fruit. Bush fruits such as gooseberries and the currants can often be bought trained as standard, a bushy head on a long stem. These have an air of

Above *Hung with glossy cherries and under planted with dazzling, orange trailing nasturtiums, this 'Morello' cherry tree makes a striking display for a shady corner. In the spring the froth of pretty white cherry blossoms that garland the tree's branches is equally eye-catching.*

Left *This ancient gnarled grape vine has had a former life in a commercial vineyard. Past its best commercially, it will still give years of good service in a garden. This solid homemade container has plenty of room for the vine and an under planting of strawberry plants.*

Above *This quirky planting has real style and personality.*

formality and sophistication which look striking when set in rows or used to flank doorways. These standard bushes can be under-planted with herbs or strawberries. These standards are not just ornaments, they can be amazingly productive, so much so that the heads can need supporting when they are laden with fruit.

choosing containers

Almost anything will do as a container, as long as it will hold soil, has a drainage hole and is about the right size. Pots which have a fatter midriff than opening at the top are best avoided as it is impossible to get plants out with their root balls unscathed when the time comes for potting on. Some pots are better at retaining moisture than others. Terracotta is porous and water evaporates through the body of the pot. Glazed, ceramic or plastic pots will lose less water. To combat water loss terracotta pots can be lined with a thick layer of newspaper. This layer of insulation also helps to keep the roots cool. In areas that suffer from heavy frosts it is best to choose frost proof pots that will not disintegrate after a couple of cold snaps. Pots labelled 'frost resistant' are not the same as frost proof, and there is no guarantee they will come through unscathed.

When choosing pots, it helps to settle on a theme. Containers do not need to 'match'. In fact, it will actually look better if they work together in a less obvious and more imaginative way. The choices are almost endless. Reclaimed and recycled objects can make both the most thrifty and interesting containers. Whatever you settle on, a few moments taken in planning your choice of pots will make a great difference to the appeal of the garden.

Initially a tree's or bush's first pot should only be a few centimetres larger in diameter than the spread of its root ball, and each year it should be moved to a larger pot. Jumping from a small pot to a much larger one is generally deemed to be unwise. This is known as over-potting. However you may have bought the ideal, large, statement pots for your terrace, and plants do have more impact in large pots. In this case keep the plant in an appropriately sized pot and conceal the pot holding the plant in the larger one until the plant is large enough to be housed in the large pot alone.

planting containers

One of the advantages of container growing fruit is that the compost you use can be exactly matched to the plant. As a general rule, soft fruits are best grown in John Innes number two, and fruit trees in John Innes number three. Acid-loving plants such as blueberries and cranberries should be planted in ericaceous compost, while strawberries are fine in multipurpose compost as they are not long lived plants.

If you are planting bareroot plants, soak the roots in a bucket of water for an hour or so before planting. With container grown plants gently tease out the root ball a little, but essentially the root ball should be left intact. Put some compost into the pot, set the plant on the compost and check that the top of the root ball or soil mark falls about 3 cm (1¼ in) below the lip of the pot. Fill the container with compost, firming as you go so the plant is held firmly in the pot. Finally water the pot thoroughly. For light pots containing tall plants that may catch the wind, a brick or something similar in the base of the pot adds weight and increases stability, though it also occupies growing space.

repotting and top dressing

As the fruit plant grows it will need more space, so each autumn it can be moved to a pot just a few centimetres larger than its last until it has finished growing, or in the case of something like a fig, until potting on becomes impractical. Knock the plant out of the pot, trim back the roots a little, gently tease out the root ball and replant it in the larger pot. If you don't get around to potting plants on one year, they will survive but there will probably be a check in their growth. Just as you would put mulch around fruiting plants in the garden, the same applies to container grown fruit. Put a 2–3 cm (¾–1¼ in) layer of a good organic mulch on the top of the potting compost.

watering and feeding container grown fruit

It is vital to keep container-grown fruit well watered, but it is equally important to avoid waterlogging. Both will affect growth and fruit production. Throughout the summer pots will need watering perhaps twice a day in extremely hot weather, though more commonly once. In the winter little water will be needed. Check the compost to see if the plant needs water – actually poke your finger a few centimetres into the compost to get a good idea of how damp the compost is at the plant's roots.

One of the problems with overwatering is that nutrients are quickly leached from the compost and so feeding is vital. Fruit plants in pots need feeding from the minute they start to grow to the moment their fruit begins to ripen. There are many liquid feeds designed specifically for growing fruit. They are high in potassium which promotes flowering and fruit formation. Choose one of these and use it in accordance with the manufacturer's instructions.

Above *One of these maiden whips will grow happily in this 23 cm (9 in) terracotta pot filled with John Innes No 3.*

the fruitful flowerbed

If you are lucky enough to possess a well-designed and planted garden then the easiest way to start growing fruit may be to add fruitful plants into existing beds or create new beds that combine fruit bushes with shrubs and perennials. Stashing fruiting plants around the garden like this has a real benefit when it comes to warding off pests and diseases; they are much less likely to be drawn to fruit hidden in amongst other plants. Mono cultures, areas of one plant species, are always more prone to attack and disease spreads rapidly from one plant to the next. Many fruit plants are good-looking enough to convincingly pull off a role centre stage. Alternatively, some bushes will make a stalwart and productive chorus line, planted behind flowering perennials that have a bit more pizzazz

Strawberries make an excellent edging plant, simple, pretty flowers and shining red fruit, particularly the variety 'Viva Rosa', which has deep pink flowers. Walls, fences and sheds can be disguised stylishly with kiwi or Japanese wineberry, both have beautiful shoots and young foliage. The kiwi has small but pretty white flowers. However both are very

Below *This newly planted bed is home to jostaberry bushes playing second fiddle to sedum 'Autumn Joy', Echinacea 'Sundown' and persicaria 'Fire tail' and some wonderful rusted, twirling iron stakes. Jostaberries are good growers and these will be stooled to keep them both fruitful and compact*

vigorous so allow them plenty of space. The fig too is an excellent plant to grow against a wall – its large, robust, hand-shaped leaves are always evocative of the Mediterranean. There is no reason why these plants cannot be combined with clematis or other climbing plants, though the resulting tangle may be a challenge to prune. A sunny wall can be clothed with a grape vine. A rampant cultivar like 'Brandt' will give an abundance of small sweet grapes and a spectacular show of autumn colour or 'Boskoop Glory' will give a reliable crop. Grape vines grow so briskly they are ideally suited to covering pergolas, providing a cool green shade of translucent leaves hung with glowing bunches of grapes in the late summer.

Many blueberry bushes are excellent decorative plants, though it has to be said some are not! Many descriptions will laud a cultivar's amazing autumn colour but not mention these leaves are hung on a six foot nondescript bush for most of the year. Two of the best are 'Sunshine Blue', my favourite, a neat, rounded almost evergreen bush with pretty leaves (even when they are green), attractive blossom and masses of blueberries. It only reaches about 60-90cm tall so is an ideal subject for the front to middle of a bed. Obviously the snag is it does need acid conditions, but a pit could be created and filled with a suitable growing medium or a good sized pot sunk in the ground.

Minaret or ballerina fruit trees have plenty of potential in the garden at large as they take up so little space but make a striking vertical focal point. These are single stems where the fruit is held close to the stem, the ballerina achieves this with no pruning whatsoever. The vertical trees look fantastic clad in blossom in spring and adorned with fruit in the summer. A stately row of these look elegant, rhythmically lining a path.

conservatory fruit

Often a forging a link between house and garden it has frequently struck me that many conservatories are a missed opportunity: these days the conservatory is more a product of the need for more living space rather than the desire to grow plants as it was historically. However the advantages of the warm, sheltered growing conditions a conservatory offers to nurture tender fruit is still there. Most people have at least a couple of plants in their conservatory, how much better if they were fruitful plants!

Melon, grapes, cape gooseberries and passion fruit thrive in the heat of a conservatory while citrus trees and figs can be successfully overwintered in a frost free cool conservatory. The care of plants grown in the conservatory is much the same as for those grown in pots (see page 38).

Above *Grown on an obelisk, melons make excellent conservatory plants, scenting the air with a rich, sweet fragrance as they ripen.*

Left *Once established even a small group of trees should provide plently of apples.*

Right *Taking the time to pick apples from the tree, rather than collecting as windfall, means they are less likely to be damaged and so will keep better.*

orchards

A well-tended orchard is a magical place, regular ranks frothing with blossom in spring and heavy with fruit in late summer and autumn. Few of us are lucky enough to have space for a large scale orchard but more are likely to have a plot suitable for a small number, perhaps four or so, dwarf bush trees that can be managed in the same way. The principles applied to large orchards are also applicable to the smallest. Large commercial orchards often contain large standard trees, though smaller trees, more intensively planted, can be more productive.

The space under trees is traditionally laid to grass – this strategy makes an orchard easy to manage. The sward should contain not just grasses but clovers and other plants that will actually contribute to fertility, special seed mixes designed for orchards are available. Traditionally this sward would have been grazed by animals, but it can be mown regularly or left as rough grass which is cut just once or twice a year. Allowing ducks, chickens and geese to forage under the trees can help to keep the number of pests down. Ideally the area around the trees should be kept free of vegetation until the trees are established. Mulch can be used around the trees, a layer of organic matter or weed suppression membrane. There is also the option of planting other fruit, blackcurrants for example, amongst the trees. Companion planting can also be used to make the orchard a healthier place (see pages 199–201).

Select a good spot for your orchard, whatever its size. Avoid natural dips or frost pockets where cold air collects making the spot more prone to frosts. Avoid exposed slopes that take the brunt of rain and the prevailing wind.

The long uninterrupted rows of trees with their interesting shifting patterns in commercial orchards are the product of convenience, tractors and machinery can move easily between the trees on the tracks left between the rows. In a domestic setting a more efficient use of space may be to pack trees closer together in offset rows with just the minimum space between them. How about a neat quincunx of trees in the lawn, you can still call it an orchard!

Commercial orchards also tend to have uninterrupted rows of trees of one variety. Again this is convenient as the fruit can all be harvested at a similar time. In your own orchard you might include one or two trees of several culvivars so the harvest will stretch from late summer through to late winter. Choosing cultivars that will pollinate each other will ensure a good yield.

what to grow

Choosing which fruit to grow and which cultivars to select is an exciting, enjoyable part of the planning process. What you choose will determine how much time and effort you will need to put in to receive a reasonable harvest in return. How much pruning will be required, when fruit will be ready to harvest, how many defences you will need to construct against attack by birds, whether you will need to protect blossom from frost and how likely you are to have to grapple with pests and diseases are all considerations.

soft fruit

Perhaps the most indulgent of fruits are the succulent, richly coloured berries and currants collectively known as soft fruits. Thankfully the fragile, flavoursome berries are easy to grow and, once established, will provide an abundance of fruit for very little effort for perhaps 10 years. Some should even provide a tantalising minor harvest in their first year – a taste of the riches to come.

Being easy to grow is not their only merit. The quality and intensity of flavour of home-produced berries and currants should far exceed those sold at premium prices in the shops. The delicate nature of soft fruit means its quality is hard to maintain in transportation (especially raspberries). A great deal of packaging is required to protect the fruit and the quality of the fruit declines rapidly once picked. The soft fruits are not only a gourmet treat, they are packed with vitamins and health-promoting phytochemicals.

The soft fruits are in reality a diverse group of plants, but can be roughly and usefully divided into two groups:

Cane fruits Raspberries, loganberries and blackberries and their numerous hybrids.

Bush fruits Gooseberries, the currants, blueberries and cranberries, with strawberries, an herbaceous plant, being the exception.

In general they all thrive in a sunny, sheltered location but the plants will tolerate a little shade, especially if they see the sun for the second part of the day. A warm, sunny location produces the sweetest, best flavoured fruits. Soft fruits in general do not do well in climates with an excessively high rainfall, as botrytis becomes a problem and the fruit is damaged. In smaller gardens soft fruits are a great way to grow your own as they will give a good amount of fruit from a few plants that need not occupy much space. Cane fruits will flourish when grown against sunny walls or fences, or can be trained over arches or obelisks to make the most of the space available. The bush fruits can be slotted into any ornamental shrub bed so long as they receive enough light, while strawberries come in forms pretty enough to edge flower beds. A better approach is to consider your space, including fences and walls. Look at the likely yields of each plant on the following pages and grow a useful number of plants of the fruit you love to eat.

Few, I hope, are unfortunate enough to have a garden without birds, and this is the major problem in growing soft fruit. There is no point trying to grow soft fruits unless you protect your fruit from the birds. They will feast on currants and berries long before you will consider them ripe. It is almost as if they watch, waiting for fruit to be just ripe enough and it will be gone almost overnight. Protecting your much-anticipated harvest need not necessitate building an elaborate fruit cage (see page 29). Flinging some mesh over the plants once the fruits form will suffice, so long as it is secure and they can't peck through at the fruit. I lost a fantastic crop of redcurrants on plants grown as cordons as I pulled the net too tightly. The bumper crop of gleaming berries were there one day and literally gone the next. Use a rigid plastic net with small square holes. Birds become horribly tangled in more flimsy cotton-type nets.

Left *Soft fruits come in a marvellous array of colours, textures and flavours, and many are sweet enough to eat straight from the bush or cane. Not only do they taste great, many contain high levels of health-promoting phytochemicals.*

blackcurrant

The cutting, tart flavour of blackcurrants makes them arguably the best soft fruit for jams, jellies and puddings. The whole plant – fruit, stems and leaves – is wonderfully aromatic, just brushing past the plants throws up a wonderful scent. They are easy to grow, a 'plant them and leave them' bush with a straightforward pruning regime. The berries are packed with vitamin C and anthocyanins, which promote antioxidant activity. However if space is limited this might be one to leave out, purely because the fruit is not as versatile as other soft fruits, unless, of course, you are an avid jam maker and they are personal favourite.

Right *Blackcurrant 'Big Ben' is known for producing huge, juicy fruits early in the season. It is also resistant to mildew and leaf spot.*

approximate yield

4.5 kg (10 lb).

fruitful years

10–15 years.

cultivars

'Ben Connan' and **'Ben Sarek'** Good choices if you are short on space as they can be planted 1.2 m (4 ft) apart.
'Ben Gairn' Has some resistance to reversion disease.
'Ben Hope' Resistant to 'big bud' (gall) mite, rust, and leaf spot and mildew and gives a good reliable crop.
Titania Good resistance to mildew and rust. Produces a large crop of good sized fruit.
'Ben Tirran' Very late to flower and fruit, making it particularly suited to colder areas that suffer from late frosts.

spacing

1.5 m (5 ft) between bushes.

planting

Plant these bushes deeper than they were grown in the nursery. The original soil level should be about 5 cm (2 in) below the surface of the soil. This is to encourage the plants to throw up new young shoots, which will bear fruit. If planting bareroot plants in late winter the stems should be cut back to about 5 cm (2 in) above soil level. If planted earlier, in the autumn, I leave the shoots untouched and enjoy a small, treasured first harvest. As with container-grown plants, set the bushes 5 cm (2 in) deeper than they were grown in the nursery. Container-grown plants do not require pruning after planting.

soil and situation

If you suffer from poorly drained soil, have a boggy corner to plant or have only a slightly shady plot, then the blackcurrant is probably one of your best chances of growing soft fruit. They are one of the plants that can be planted under standard fruit trees making a good use of space. Obviously they will do better given more favourable conditions – a rich, fertile, moist soil in a reasonably sunny spot will give the best crop.

maintenance

A generous layer of garden compost or well-rotted manure in the spring and perhaps a handful or two of pelleted poultry manure is all that is required. Blackcurrants can be quite hungry bushes and the nitrogen-rich feed will encourage plenty of new fruit-bearing growth – essential if you are cutting the bushes back to ground level.

blackcurrant

pruning

Fruits mostly on last season's wood and also crops on older wood. Blackcurrants are reasonably forgiving of neglected pruning. There is no need to prune until the bush is a couple of years old. During the winter, cut out about one third of the oldest branches (these are easy to spot as they will be the thickest and have the darkest bark) close to the bottom of the bush. Also take out any dead or diseased wood.

An easier method is to cut back the entire bush every three years. If you have a number of bushes this can be done in rotation, ensuring you still get a crop each year. If you grow six bushes then each year two will be cut to the ground completely, leaving the other four to fruit.

Left *There will be currants at all stages of ripeness on a single bush. Only pick those that have become black a few days earlier.*

when to harvest

Once the fruit turns a shiny black, leave it another few days and then the tart currants will be ready to enjoy. The berries make good jam, jellies and wine and freeze well. They don't collapse quite as badly as other soft fruit which has been frozen.

problems and solutions

Birds stealing the currants is much less of a problem than other soft fruits. However if the fruits are left on the bushes for too long, or there is nothing else available for them to feast upon, they will strip the bush clean.

Big bud is most noticeable in the spring, when gall mites living inside the buds cause them to grow larger and rounder than they should. These mites spread reversion disease that leads to an extremely reduced fruit crop. The only course of action is to cut off the affected growth and burn it. There are good varieties which show resistance to big bud, such as Ben Hope, and Ben Gairn is resistant to reversion disease. In allotments where reversion disease can be widespread these resistant varieties are a good choice.

jostaberry

The jostaberry is a hybrid between the gooseberry and blackcurrant. The berries are glorious and look like an over-sized blackcurrant with a similar flavour, but which devotees describe as more appealing. The plants make prodigious vegetative growth and usually crop well if you can keep the birds off. Their vigour means they can be allowed to grow to enormous proportions, or be kept as standards and even planted as a hedge. To keep them smaller they can be grown as stooled bushes like the blackcurrant and completely cut to the ground every third year, or a third of the oldest branches removed each year. The fruit makes tasty jam and freezes well. This hybrid is really robust and fairly problem free.

Left *The juicy berries of the jostaberry look wonderful and taste delicious.*

redcurrant

Redcurrants are arguably the most beautifully seductive of the soft fruits. While they look mouth-wateringly delicious, however, as with blackcurrants they are really just for cooks. Besides their role as a fine dining garnish, redcurrants are not good to eat raw, but make good jellies and preserves and mix well with other fruits such as raspberries. They are simple to grow and are treated more like gooseberries than the blackcurrants.

approximate yield

3.5–4.5 kg (8–10 lb) when grown as a bush, 1–1.5 kg (2–3 lb) when grown as a cordon

fruitful years

10 years.

cultivars

'Jonkheer Van Tets' The earliest of the redcurrants, it produces an exceptionally abundant crop of excellently flavoured large fruit.

'Rovada' Produces a very heavy yield late in the season, strong growing upright bush and good disease resistance. It flowers later than most and so makes a good choice for colder regions where flowers might get nipped by frost.

spacing

Redcurrants can be grown as a bush, a cordon or double cordon. Bushes will provide a bigger crop but cordons offer a space saving option and can be supported on wire or grown against walls or fences. Cordons are straightforward to prune. Bushes need about 1.2–1.5 m (4–5 ft) of space between bushes. Cordons can be planted at about 30 cm (12 in) apart and double cordons at 60–70 cm (24–27½ in) apart.

planting

Bareroot bushes and cordons can be planted throughout the winter, so long as the ground is not frozen. To give plants the best possible start, plant as soon as the bushes become available in late autumn. Container grown plants can be planted at anytime but will be less of a burden if planted in late autumn. Redcurrant bushes are grown on a short leg (like a trunk) so the bushes should be planted at the same level as they were growing in the container or nursery bed.

soil and situation

Redcurrants will grow best in sheltered location, in fertile soil. Cordons will grow against a north facing wall but will do better in a warmer spot. Without the warmth of the sun the fruit will be even sharper than you might expect.

maintenance

Apply a good layer of mulch annually and water in dry spells when the fruit is swelling to ensure good sized fruit.

pruning

Tackle bushes during the winter dormant period and cordons after the fruit has been picked. Redcurrant bushes are very forgiving of misjudged pruning and will grow back vigorously. Redcurrants produce fruit at the base of the previous year's growth – bear this in mind and the pruning strategy should make sense.

Right *Redcurrant 'Jonkheer Van Tets'.*

redcurrant

Bush Grown as a bush, the aim is to achieve an open goblet shape on a short leg (like a trunk of a few centimetres) and so they are pruned in the same way as gooseberries. It is simplest to prune in three stages:

1. Take out any dead wood and remove branches that are crowding the centre.
2. Cut back all the main stems by half.
3. Finally trim back side shoots to about 5 cm (2 in) to an upward-facing bud.

Cordons It may seem that cordons might be difficult to prune, but in fact it is a quick and simple task. After the fruit has been picked, cut side shoots back to about 7 cm (3 in) – the side shoots are the twiggy growth from the spurs, which are the branches which grow from the main stem.

Above *Redcurrant 'Rovada' trained as cordons just coming into leaf in their first year in the garden. These were bought already trained and, unlike some restricted forms, should be simple to maintain. Prune the side shoots to leave just five leaves on each in the summer, cut the laterals back to a bud about 2.5 cm (1 in) or so and trim the leader (the main vertical stem) to leave about 13 cm (5 in) of new growth in the winter.*

when to harvest

The currants turn red before they are quite ripe. Watch as they deepen in colour – that is the moment they are ripe. Whole strigs (this is the name for a bunch of currants) should ripen at about the same time and so the best way to harvest is to gently pull upwards and remove the whole strig from the plant. The individual currants can be either picked off later or removed by pulling the strig through a large fork. There are picking devices available that claim to hasten the harvesting process, like a large metal comb attached to a scoop, which acts as a collection hopper that is run through the dangling strigs, removing the currants and catching them in the scoop. This may be worthwhile if you have a great many currants and berries to harvest, though it may be a little indiscriminate where fruit are ripening at different times.

problems and solutions

The redcurrant blister aphid, as its name helpfully suggests, causes red blisters on the leaves of redcurrants as the insects cluster underneath the young leaves. To tackle the problem, cut the off the affected shoots and destroy them once the fruit has set.

Leaf spot and **coral spot** may also be a problem.

Below *Redcurrant 'Rovada'.*

white currant

Growing and caring for white currants is much the same as for redcurrants. These berries, which are probably more accurately described as a warm cream or pale yellow when ripe, are in fact a sport of the redcurrant but have not inherited the redcurrant's sharp taste – they are much sweeter.

approximate yield

2.5–5.5 kg (5½–12 lb) when grown as a bush, 1.5 kg (3 lb) as a cordon.

fruitful years

10–15 years.

cultivars

'Blanka' Good sized fruits held in long strigs in profusion. This cultivar promises the best yields possible.

'White Versailles' An old variety. If you plan on just one bush its sweet, large fruit and reliability make this the one to choose.

Above *Though not as glamorous-looking as the red-currant, the white currant is still delicious and less tart.*

gooseberry

Soft, plump dessert gooseberries are a real treat, as good to eat straight from the bush as any strawberry or grape. It is amazing that something so luxurious in both size and flavour can grow on such a robust, spiny and forgiving bush. As with all fruit, gooseberries will produce more and better fruit when they are grown well. They will, however, fruit their way through years of neglect. A good layer of mulch and some straightforward pruning, and the results should be great. Culinary gooseberries are much more tart and astringent than dessert varieties. For most gardeners it pays to keep things simple and and grow just the luscious dessert and culinary varieties, taking under-ripe berries early in the summer for cooking.

Left *Quite deservedly, one of the most frequently grown gooseberries 'Invicta' is a real stalwart.*

approximate yield

3.5–4.5 kg (8–10 lb) per bush.

fruitful years

Approximately 10 years.

cultivars

'Hinnomaki Red' A good yield of large red fruit. This bush has good mildew resistance. Culinary and dessert variety.

'Hinnomaki Yellow' An excellent dessert cultivar, this plant produces large, warm yellow fruits on a robust bush with good mildew resistance.

'Invicta' Very commonly grown variety, probably because it is reliable, vigorous, produces a hefty crop and is resistant to mildew. The only slight negative is the bushes are very prickly. Culinary and dessert variety.

'Pax' Produces a more compact bush than Invicta and can be planted just 1.25 m (4 ft) apart. It has good resistance to mildew and, being spineless, the large red berries it produces are easy to pick. Culinary and dessert variety.

planting and spacing

Plants grown in bush form can be grown about 1.2 to 1.5 m (4–5 ft) apart, cordons about 30 cm (12 in) apart. Plant bareroot bushes during the dormant period so that the soil level is at the same as that the bush was originally grown in – the soil mark should be clearly visible on the stem. Container grown bushes can be planted at anytime of year but will establish more quickly and be easier to manage if planted in the late autumn.

soil and situation

If you have a sunny, reasonably sheltered spot with reasonable soil then your gooseberries will thrive. If you don't they will grow in areas that are inclined to be shady and can be successfully grown in the space under standard fruit trees. Container grown plants

Right *An excellent dual purpose gooseberry, 'Achilles' can be picked whilst green in the early summer for pies or jam making or left to become plump, sweet and the deepest shade of red later in the season. This gooseberry has good mildew resistance.*

gooseberry

will yield a worthwhile crop. Standard plants look quite handsome in their pots and can crop so heavily that their heads need supporting.

maintenance

Pile a good layer of organic mulch around the bushes and a handful of pelleted chicken manure or all purpose organic fertilizer in early spring. If you are growing dessert varieties, remove about half of the berries for cooking in early summer while they are still green and firm. This leaves space and resources for the remaining fruit to swell and ripen and form large berries later in the summer.

pruning

Prune in winter, during the dormant period.

Bush Grown as a bush, the aim is to achieve an open goblet shape on a short leg (like a trunk of a few centimetres), and so they are pruned in the same way as redcurrants. It is simplest to prune in three stages:

1. Take out any dead wood and remove branches that are crowding the centre.
2. Cut back all the main stems by half.
3. Finally trim back side shoots to about 5 cm (2 in) to an upward facing bud.

Cordons It may seem that cordons might be difficult to prune, but in fact it is a quick and simple task once you begin. After the fruit has been picked, cut side shoots back to about 7 cm (3 in) – the side shoots grow from the spurs which grow from the main stem.

when to harvest

With dessert/culinary varieties you have two harvests, although not two crops, unfortunately. Removing some fruit early in the season, in very early summer, for crumbles, pies and jam reduces overcrowding and means that those left on the bush will grow to more generous proportions and ripen well. When fully ripe the berries will give slightly when squeezed. Once picked the fruit will last perhaps one or two weeks in the fridge, and the berries freeze well.

problems and solutions

American mildew One of the biggest problems affecting gooseberry bushes. A white, powdery bloom forma on leaves and the fruit. The fruit is still edible if the powder is wiped away. The affected shoots can be removed. Pruning to open up the centre of the bush may help reduce the problem. Resistant varieties are readily available, and all of the cultivars listed above have good resistance to mildew. Undoubtedly the easiest option is to grow one of these. Older popular varieties such as 'Winham's Industry' or 'Leveller may have excellent fruit, but they have no resistance to this common problem.

Gooseberry sawfly This is one of the most difficult problems I have had to overcome in growing gooseberries. In fact I am not entirely sure I did completely triumph, but rather made things tolerable. The 2.5 cm (1 in) long dull grey-green caterpillars inhabit the underside of the gooseberry leaves and look fairly harmless, but in great numbers can strip a bush of leaves in days – piranha like in their ruthless efficiency. A small bush in its first year defoliated in this manner may well die. The only solution is to remove the caterpillars by hand as soon as you see them.

Birds Will leave hard, green culinary berries alone. The tender dessert varieties might be attractive to them once ripe but they are not a big draw.

Left *Remarkably this little bush is in its first year, planted bareroot just a few months earlier. Many people would have stripped off the immature fruit, but I could not resist enjoying this exciting if modest harvest.*

blueberry

Hailed as a 'superfood', the blueberry has magnificent nutritional credentials – high in fibre, vitamins A and C, magnesium, potassium, iron and antioxidant phytonutrients. Researchers have suggested they have a whole array of disease and age-beating qualities, but perhaps best of all they are an absolute pleasure to eat and child's play to grow, so long as you get the soil right. The berries are blue-black to deep purple in colour and sport a dusty white bloom. The flavour can range from incredibly sweet, where berries are a treat straight from the bush, to others that are tangy and tart and best kept for cooking in pies or preserves.

Like cranberries, blueberries are heathland plants and require an acidic soil with a pH of 4–5.5 and plenty of moisture. The good news is that if your soil is not suitable then blueberries grow well in containers where you can easily control the acidity of the soil. Some like the compact 'Sunshine Blue' make excellent subjects for containers, as they are very attractive with pretty pink flowers, firey autumn colours and semi-evergreen foliage as well as being staggeringly productive.

approximate yield

4.5–9 kg (10–20 lb).

fruitful years

Varies according to conditions.

cultivars

There is a wide variation in the habit of different blueberry cultivars depending on whether they have high bush or low bush ancestry. Low bush plants tend to tolerate less acidity and water than high bush cultivars. Many are self-fertile but a better crop is achieved if cross-pollination is possible, so it makes sense to grow more than one cultivar.

'Patriot' A cultivar specifically bred to thrive in colder areas, it consistently produces a heavy crop of large, tasty berries. The bushes reach about 1.2 m (4 ft) high and are spreading in their habit. Attractive white flowers and good autumn colour means this bush holds its own amongst ornamental shrubs. Early.

'Sunshine Blue' Wonderfully compact, neat looking bushes and the only completely self-fertile cultivar. Rounded bushes grow to about 60–90 cm (24–36 in) and produce good sized sweet berries. Mid season.

'Earliblue' This makes a large bush when mature, about 1.8 m (6 ft) tall. It produces plenty of large sweet berries. Early.

'Chandler' Has the great advantage of producing large, sweet berries over a very long period, quite possibly 8 weeks or so from midsummer. It is a fairly large plant reaching 1.5 m (5 ft) tall.

'Bluecrop' This upright bush reaches about 1.8 m (6 ft) tall, not an attractive bush but it is arguably the most productive. It produces an outstanding crop of large, very tasty berries. Self-fertile. Mid season.

Right *Blueberry 'Patriot'.*

blueberry

Above *'Ivanhoe' is a strong growing blueberry with an erect form.*

planting and spacing

Blueberry cultivars vary greatly in size, some are up to 1.8 m (6 ft) in height. These are the high bush varieties descended from the American wild blueberry. Smaller more compact cultivars only reach 90 cm (36 in) tall. Larger bushes should be spaced about 1.5 m (5 ft) apart and will grow happily in a half barrel sized pot when mature. Smaller cultivars should do well set just 1 m (3 ft) apart.

Blueberries are available as container-grown plants and are best planted in the early autumn, but can be added to the garden at any time of year so long as they are kept well watered. The plants should be planted in the ground so that the soil level is the same as in the pot.

soil and situation

An acidic soil or growing medium is essential. If you are unsure about the whether your soil is acid or alkaline, garden centres sell simple pH testing kits. The tests are straightforward to carry out and will give you an important piece of information about growing conditions in your garden. In containers, ericaceaous compost (available in sacks from the garden centre) or a mix of peat, sand and leafmould can be used. You can increase the acidity of your soil by digging in acidic material to a depth of about 60 cm (24 in). Over time the acidity will decline and it may be necessary to apply flowers of sulphur to return the balance. Alternatively, build a raised bed and fill it as you would a container. Blueberries appreciate a sunny, sheltered site but will tolerate some shade.

maintenance

Blueberries are not hard to keep but their requirements are just a little different to the rest of the fruit garden. Blueberries will not welcome the good layer of compost or manure that the annual mulch provides. Instead they need a good wodge of partially rotted pine, sawdust or pine needles. These plants do require plenty of water, though low bush varieties are more tolerant of dryer soils than the high bush types. Keeping the surface of the soil well covered with mulch helps retain moisture. They should only be

irrigated with rain water – consistently watering with limy tap water will damage the plants. If the water butts have run dry, watering a couple of times with tap water is better than the plants becoming stressed though lack of water.

Removing all the fruiting buds (these are the fat rounded buds) from newly planted bushes is one way of ensuring greater harvests in later years. This means no harvest in your first year – pain now for gain later. I am unable to resist the temptation of a small harvest the first year, and if bushes look over burdened with fruit as they form I might remove a portion. Harvests are still good, but of course I have no way of knowing how much better they might have been!

pruning

Blueberries need no pruning. They can be planted and left pretty much to their own devices. Simply remove any dead or damaged growth.

when to harvest

Unripe berries are incredibly sharp. Wait until the berries are fully coloured, have a good bloom on them and look fit to burst, then they are ripe and should come away from the plant easily. If the berries begin to lose their plumpness, you have missed the point of perfection. The berries will ripen over a number of weeks and keep well in the refrigerator for longer than many soft fruits, which is nice if you enjoy eating them fresh. When you have a glut the berries freeze well. Freezing affects the taste a little but preserves all the valuable nutrients. Their distinctive flavour makes for excellent pies and preserves.

Above left *It is fortunate that blueberry 'Duke' is reputed to keep better than other blueberries as it produces an exceptionally heavy crop year after year.*

Above right *'Spartan' produces tangy fruits early in the summer on a bush that reaches about 1.8 m (6 ft).*

pests and diseases

Blueberries are exceptional in having no significant problems with pests and diseases. The main enemy of the blueberry grower is the birds as they adore them, beginning their onslaught even before the berries are near ripe, so netting is absolutely essential.

cranberry

In many ways cranberries are like their close relatives the blueberry, but for me they lack the taste and joy that makes it worth modifying growing conditions for them. In fact, unless you garden in an acidic bog, then the only way to grow cranberries is to create one or simulate bog-type conditions in a container. Once that is sorted out they are not hard to grow, and they contain a good range of beneficial nutrients. They are not the type of sweet berry that can be plucked from the plant and savoured – they are for cooking and preserves.

approximate yield

2.25 kg (5 lb).

fruitful years

Only 3 or 4 in a container, longer in the ground.

cultivars

Cranberries are ususally just labelled as cranberries, not as named cultivars. Only buy **'Vaccinium macrocarpan'**, the American cranberry, which produces large berries, not the British native **'Vaccinium oxycoccus'**.

planting and spacing

Cranberries are usually only available as container grown plants. They often appear in nurseries when they are smothered in berries as they look incredibly appealing. Plants should be planted with the soil at the same level as in the pot they have been grown in, about 30–45 cm (12–17¾ in) apart.

soil and situation

Cranberries need acidic, damp soil. To create the perfect conditions for about 5 or 6 plants dig out an area about a meter/yard square and 25 cm (10 in) deep. Line it with plastic and poke a small few holes in it. Fill the lined holes with a combination of sand, leaf mould, acidic soil and sawdust, and mix well. Slightly over-fill the bed as the level will drop as the material settles. You have to really want those cranberries. In containers use ericaceous compost and restrict the drainage by plugging the drainage holes, or sit the pot in a saucer. If you have acidic soil they can be grown as marginal plants around a pond or a bog area created as above, but you can refill with your own garden soil.

maintenance

Cranberries require copious amounts of rainwater. The soil should be very moist at all times but don't drown the plants.

pruning

No pruning is needed. The bushes can be trimmed and tidied after fruiting.

when to harvest

The berries are undeniably tempting when they are ripe in early autumn. Ripe berries keep well in the refrigerator, perhaps up to 2 months, or can be frozen. Ripe cranberries bounce, caused by air pockets within the fruit. Commercial growers have used the ability of the ripe cranberry to bounce as a method of sorting unripe and damaged from those fit for sale.

pests and diseases

None to speak of. Sickly plants are most likely to be caused by a lack of acidity or water.

Right *All cranberries should be harvested before the first frosts.*

blackberry

The stalwart berry of the late summer and autumn, the enormous, glossy, cultivated blackberry is far more eye-catching and glamorous than the fruits of hedgerow bramble. The garden cultivars are much less unruly than the hedgerow ruffian. Many are thornless, with a compact habit, and some even have prettily shaped leaves. The garden types are still tough enough to make them the easiest soft fruit to grow. They are undemanding, unfussy and have few problems to occupy the gardener. They take up little growing space and can be grown up fences, trellises or more rampant cultivars can even be used to disguise sheds or out buildings. And, of course, the berries are fantastic to eat.

Left *Many garden blackberry cultivars produce much larger, plumper berries than those found in the hedgerows.*

approximate yield

6.75–13.5 kg (15–30 lb).

fruitful years

15 to 20 (known to be 25 years plus in the wild).

cultivars

'Silvan' Will produce a good crop of well-sized berries, even on heavy soils. Will tolerate drought, too, and has a good resistance to disease.

'Oregon Thornless' Ideal for small spaces, this thornless variety has prettily shaped leaves which add to its appeal. The berries it produces are sweet but not the largest. It crops less prolifically than most others but if you want something pretty, fruitful and easy to prune, it is worth growing. Needs about 3 m (10 ft) of wall or wires.

'Waldo' A small plant that will be happy trained up a single post or cane wigwam to save space. It is resistant to cane and leaf spot, and the fruit are large with an excellent flavour. I have always found it a little slow to get going.

'Himalaya Giant' This is a bit of a thug – it is very vigorous and spiny. If you have a fence you don't want climbed then this is the solution. It can even be grown on posts and wires to create a windbreak. The yield is equally impressive but the berries are best for cooking. Allow each plant a good 5 m (16 ft).

'Loch Tay' Produces a profusion of small but very sweet berries. It has no thorns and has a neat, compact habit making it good for small spaces. If you want to grow more than one plant, they can be set just 1–1.5 m (3–5 ft) apart.

spacing

The space between plants depends on the cultivar– 5 m (16 ft) for a vigorous cultivar like Himalayan Giant and just 1 m (3 ft) for the smallest.

planting

Blackberries are available as bareroot plants in the dormant season, and container plants for most of the year. Container-grown plants are best planted in early autumn. Plants should be set so the new soil level is the same as it was in the pot or nursery bed. Blackberries need some form of support. Wires can be strung along a wall or fence, or from stout posts set securely in the ground. Ideally the support should be about 2 m (6½ ft) tall with wires set about 30 cm (11¾ in) apart starting about 90 cm (35 in) from the ground.

Right *Blackberry 'Black Bute'.*

blackberry

soil and situation

These plants are very unfussy, so long as the site is not waterlogged. A sunny spot will give the sweetest fruit, but they will grow happily in partial shade.

maintenance

A good layer of organic mulch in early spring and perhaps a handful of all purpose fertilizer is all that is needed.

pruning

After fruiting and before late spring. The blackberry fruits mostly on the previous season's growth, so pruning simply removes all canes that have borne fruit leaving the fresh new canes to fruit the following season.

As with raspberries (see page 81) this is very straightforward. All the canes which produce fruit should be cut out at ground level. Vigorous, spiky cultivars can put up a bit of a fight and so it is best to wear stout gloves and long sleeves. Training all one season's growth in one direction along horizontal wires and the following season's growth in the opposite direction can help avoid tangles. The canes are much more flexible than raspberries and so are easily twisted to be positioned just where they are needed without snapping. I often just spiral the new growth around the wires rather than bothering with ties or twine.

Above *The smooth stems of 'Oregon thornless' make both picking and pruning a great deal less painful than the incredibly spiky cultivars.*

when to harvest

Wait until the berries are fully coloured. The berries on a single plant will ripen over a period of weeks so it will be necessary to pick several times. Once bushes are established there are almost certainly be more berries than you can eat, these can be frozen by the tray method (see page 208). Though they collapse after freezing they still make great, if slightly seedy, jam, jellies, wines and liqueurs.

pests and diseases

Birds should be the only problem. Net the bushes as soon as the fruit is formed, though if you have a good crop there should be plenty left for you.

Left *Blackberry 'Silvan' is a reliable cultivar, tolerating heavy soil and drought.*

hybrid berries

There are many hybrid berries available. The product of crossing two, or even three, berries to produce a plant and fruit with a slightly different characteristic than the parents.

Above *The large, juicy berries produced by the olalliberry make excellent preserves.*

Right *These tayberries are yet to achieve the deep maroon colour which indicates they are ripe and ready for picking.*

tayberry *Raspberry x blackberry*

Sweet, flavoursome, large berries are produced by this rather thorney plant. The berries are a deep, dusty red when ripe. Not as hardy as other hybrids, the tayberry may get nipped by frost in exposed locations. Plant 2.5 m (8 ft) apart.

loganberry *Raspberry x blackberry*

Ripening in midsummer, the dark red fruit of the loganberry looks rather like a stretched raspberry. They are sharp-tasting and suited to cooking and jam making. These are vigorous plants, which throw up a forest of new canes each year. There are two types – LY59 and LY654 (thornless and grows less strongly).

boysenberry *Loganberry x blackberry x raspberry*

Thornless and plump, the elongated berries are fantastic for jam making. This hybrid requires a warmer site to thrive than other berry hybrids and is better able to survive periods of drought.

olalliberry *Loganberry x young berry*

This berry tastes, looks and behaves much like a blackberry, although the berries are generally larger and sweeter.

pruning

Prune in winter. Most fruit is produced on last summer's growth, so like raspberries and blackberries the best policy is to remove all the canes that have produced fruit to ground level. They will fruit a little on canes in their third year like blackberries and raspberries, so neglected pruning one year is not a problem. However it does make removing all the spent canes the following year more time consuming.

raspberry

Raspberries are one of those marvellous fruits that are a real treat to eat, give enormous rewards for the space they occupy in the garden and are amazingly easy to grow. Minimum care should yield basket loads of sweet, fresh tasting fruits. Growing your own means you can pick the berries when they are perfectly ripe and enjoy the best possible flavour. They will usually bear fruit the season after planting.

Perfectly ripe, tender raspberries would never survive the journey to supermarket and home again undamaged. If you grow two or three cultivars that fruit at different times you can stretch the raspberry harvest. Grow autumn fruiting cultivars too and you can be enjoying these wonderful fruits up until the first frost.

approximate yield

1 kg (2 lb) per 30 cm (12 in) of canes.

fruitful years

After 10 years plants become less productive and badly affected by viruses.

cultivars

Early

'Glen Moy' This is an excellent early cultivar that delivers an abundant crop of good-sized berries on spineless canes. In warmer areas this marvellous plant might also deliver a small autumn crop. Resistant to greenfly.

'Malling Jewel' An old favourite that has an excellent flavour and boasts good resistance to virus infection. Gives a good yield but is not as prolific as some. Once ripe, the berries can remain on the plant a while without spoiling – a boon for gardeners who cannot visit their garden frequently or grow on an allotment.

Above *The unusual, delicate pink-tinged apricot fruits of raspberry 'Valentina' belie its tough constitution, as it has good resistance to pests and diseases.*

Left *Raspberry 'Tulameen'.*

Midsummer

'Glen Ample' produces large, well-flavoured berries in good number and has good disease resistance.

Late Summer

'Glen Prosen' This variety promises a bumper harvest every time, though it is a little fussier than most and not a good choice if your soil is poor. The plants are resistant to aphids and virus and spine free.

'Malling Admiral' This robust raspberry has excellent disease resistance and produces an abundance of good sized, dark red, delicious berries. This cultivar is often referred to as the ideal raspberry, so if you plan to grow just one cultivar try this one.

Left *Old raspberry canes are cut off at ground level.*

raspberry

spacing

Plant canes about 30–45 cm (12–18 in) apart. Canes are usually available in bundles of five, and when planted over a 1.5–2 m (5–6½ ft) row could yield 5–6 kg (11–13 lb) of raspberries once established. The canes will arrive with about a 30 cm (12 in) or so length of woody stem and a tangle of roots.

Plant raspberries as bareroot canes in the dormant season – late autumn or early winter is best as it allows plants to get established while the ground is still warm – otherwise wait until late winter early spring when the weather starts to warm up.

Raspberry canes will require some form of support. The simplest method of support is horizontal wires stretched between vertical posts about 2 m (6½ ft) tall. In my fruit garden wires are spaced to suit the range of plants growing along their length. A neat row of raspberries can be used as a fruitful garden divide or boundary. They can easily be grown up a wall or existing fence, and in the past I have used them to disguise deer fencing.

The easiest way to plant raspberry canes is to dig a narrow trench about 8 cm (3 in) deep, place the canes in the trench at intervals of about 30–45 cm (12–17¾ in) and back fill the trench firming the soil as you go. Ensure the canes are standing up and the soil level is the same as they were grown in the nursery. Cut the canes back to 30 cm (12 in) if the canes are significantly longer. The exceptions are plants bought specifically as long canes. In the hope of getting a harvest in the first season these should be left just as they are. As an impatient gardener by nature, I have tried these and found them tricky to establish, though that may have been down to the cultivar 'Tulameen'.

soil and situation

Raspberries enjoy a humus rich, well drained but moisture-retentive soil, though they are reasonably tolerant of less than perfect conditions. They will thrive in a warm, sunny location but will take some shade. Unless you live in a very hot climate when some shade might be helpful, a sunny spot will give the best, sweetest harvest.

maintenance

There is really very little to be done apart from a good layer of mulch and a handful of multipurpose organic fertilizer in early spring, and giving the fruit some protection from the birds.

In very dry weather it may help to water as the fruit is swelling to ensure the fruits are succulent and juicy, and young plants need regular watering until they are well established.

pruning

Prune after fruit and before spring. Cut back all the old canes that have borne fruit to ground level and tie in the new canes. The old canes will look dark, tatty and carry the remains of fruit stalks. Any weak or new canes can be cut out too. There is the option of not pruning in this way, leaving the old canes to bare a little fruit in their second year. However this is one short cut which can result in more work the following year as the whole bed becomes tangled. Nevertheless it is reassuring to know that should the pruning get overlooked one year, it will not result in a poor harvest.

when to harvest

As the berries ripen, the harvest period will stretch over a number of weeks. When ripe the berry should pull cleanly away leaving the hull on the plant. If the berries collapse in your fingers that usually means they are overripe and are best eaten immediately! The berries need to eaten soon after harvest as they deteriorate quickly, even in the refrigerator. If you are lucky enough to have a glut, the berries can be made into jam, frozen or used to flavour liqueurs (see page 210).

problems and solutions

Growing disease-resistant cultivars goes a long way to making growing raspberries a trouble free experience. The main threat to your crop will probably be the birds, as they will strip the berries from the canes long before they are ripe enough to harvest. Netting is the most reliable option, though you also have to ensure the net does not lie too close to the fruit or the birds will peck through. Moving objects and sound can help deter the birds (see pages 202–203).

Raspberry beetle This pest causes a brown distorted area on the fruit near the stalk. It is a small beetle that lays its eggs in the raspberry flower and its larvae, when they hatch, eat their way into the fruit. Short term there is nothing to be done, but disturbing the life cycle of the beetle by moving the soil around the base of the plant, by hoeing say, should help the problem. Autumn fruiting cultivars do not suffer from this problem, so if the damage persists opt for one of these.

Viruses can bring plants to a point where there is little that can be done. Plants lose their vigour, look miserable and become unproductive. Once in this state, plants should be removed and destroyed. The problem is that if you re-plant raspberries in the same plot, it is likely they would soon succumb to the same viruses, so only replant in a different bed. Choosing disease resistant varieties helps stave off the inevitable, though you should get about a decade's worth of fruit before the situation demands radical action and the plants need removing.

Above *Raspberry 'Glen Ample'.*

Chlorosis This is a yellowing of the leaves caused by a lack of chlorophyll and is more likely in limy soils where a shortage of manganese and iron arises. Apply a supplement high in these elements in accordance with the manufacturer's instructions. The same symptoms can be induced by poor drainage or just less than perfect growing conditions.

autumn raspberry

If I had to choose just one fruit to grow I would be hard pressed to decide between autumn raspberries and blueberries. Both are very easy to grow and a treat to eat. The same irresistibly tasty fruits as summer fruiting varieties but even simpler to grow, autumn raspberries have the added allure of fruiting when most soft fruit is at an end. For the most part, the cultivation of autumn fruiting raspberries is the same as raspberries, except they are even less demanding as they generally need no support, do not suffer from attack by raspberry beetle and the pruning is a cinch.

cultivars

'Autumn Bliss' Perhaps the best known autumn variety, it produces large, well flavoured fruit on sturdy plants.
'Fallgold' More than just a novelty, this yellow cultivar produces a good number of tasty fruits that look very appealing. A mix of red and yellow berries in any pudding creates a real feast for the eyes.
'Joan J' Produces a good crop over a long period.
'Zeva' Has a reasonable crop of large, deep red berries. This cultivar is hardier than most and has a reputation for doing well in colder areas.

pruning

Late winter. This type of raspberry fruits on the top of the current season's growth so pruning really couldn't be simpler. Just cut down all the canes, that is the entire plant, to ground level in winter.

Above *Raspberry 'Autumn Bliss'.*

Left and right *Raspberry 'Fallgold'.*

japanese wineberry

Also known as Chinese Blackberries. Incredibly tasty, not available in the shops and dead easy to grow – perfect credentials for making them a must have in any fruit grower's garden. A member of the rubus family (others include blackberries and raspberries), the Japanese wineberry is a true species, not one of the many hybrids available, and is self-fertile. The berries are not large and can be a fiddle to harvest as the stems of the canes are covered in fine spines, but these are not as likely to damage as a thorny blackberry. The smallish berries are sweet, incredibly delicious and a glistening orange/red. I have read that the berry being held in a large calyx and the spiny stems are a deterrent to birds, although sadly not in my garden, so I recommend netting the plants if you can. The berries are quite unlike any others and best eaten straight from the plant, though they can obviously be used in the same way as other berries.

Above and left *The easily-trained stems and decorative red spines make the wineberry a useful ornamental plant.*

approximate yield

A little less than raspberries and blackberries.

fruitful years

Many.

cultivars

There are no named cultivars.

spacing

Allow 3–4 m (10–13 ft) between plants and supports should be a minimum of 2 m (6½ ft) high.

planting

Japanese wineberries need some support; they can be used to clothe fences or trellises or grown up post and wire supports. These need to be of sturdy construction as the plant can make an awful lot of growth. The reddish-brown spines and fresh green foliage of new canes is very attractive and almost seems to glow, making the wineberry a good candidate for making boundaries throughout the garden.

soil and situation

Just about anywhere will do, but given good, moist soil the fruit will be larger and more abundant.

maintenance

Give the plant a good layer of organic material in the spring.

pruning

Prune in autumn and winter. Like the raspberry and blackberry, the Japanese wineberry fruits mostly on the previous summer's growth, so simply remove all canes which have fruited and any weak or diseased canes. These are robust plants and pruning the tangle of spiny stems can be a time consuming tussle. Tie in the new growth as neatly as possible.

when to harvest

When the berries are a deep ruby red in mid to late summer.

problems and solutions

Birds are likely to be the only problem, so cover the bushes in net once the fruits are formed.

goji berry

Also known as wolfberries. Not a delicious delight like a raspberry, the goji berry has gained popularity for its famed nutritional value that is said to boost the immune system, promote longevity and give many other health benefits. The berries are usually eaten dried, though they can be used in cooking or smoothies. I cannot persuade anyone in my family to eat them, despite their great health advantages. Despite their high price in the shops, they are terrifically easy to grow, even in poor soil, they will tolerate dry spells and they are self-fertile. They are an excellent choice for anyone who wants to grow fruit with little effort so long as you enjoy them, otherwise there are plenty of nutrient-rich berries that are a real treat to eat. Though the goji berry bush will withstand cold temperatures, they are not happy in tropical climes.

Right *Once established, the goji berry bush will provide a hefty harvest.*

approximate yield

4 kg (9 lb) when 6 years old (1kg/2 lb at year 2).

fruitful years

Decades.

cultivars

Usually just sold as goji berry bushes.

spacing

About 1–1.5 m (3–5 ft) should be left between plants.

planting

Like all fruiting plants they are best planted in late autumn, though they can be added to the garden at anytime if they are container grown so long as they receive plenty of care and attention. Plant the bush at the same depth as it is in the pot.

soil and situation

These plants are really not hard to please: any reasonable soil will fit the bill, though better soil will encourage a better yield. They will tolerate some shade but will fair better in a sunny spot.

maintenance

An annual mulch of organic matter is all that is needed.

pruning

Prune in winter. There are several schools of thought on pruning the natural weeping bush habit of the easy going goji. Traditionally in Asia it was pruned to an umbrella form, or a two or three tier weeping form with a main trunk. It will still fruit well if left unpruned, though it will reach about 3 m (10 ft) in height. Pruning just to keep it in check to stop it swamping any neighbours is another option. Should a radical prune become necessary, this robust plant should respond well to being cut back hard. This is really not a fussy plant.

when to harvest

When the berries are fully coloured.

problems and solutions

The bushes should be trouble-free.

strawberry

Succulent and intensely flavoursome home-grown strawberries can be enjoyed just moments from picking, so none of the glorious sweetness is lost. They can be successfully grown in pots and are pretty enough to hold their own in ornamental flower beds, but if you have the space, creating a dedicated strawberry bed is well worthwhile. Carefully selecting the varieties planted in your garden can ensure fantastic strawberries throughout the summer and into early autumn.

There are two types of strawberry to consider when planning your garden: summer strawberries, which will have one flush of fruit and perhaps a second later in the summer, and perpetual or remontant strawberries. Don't be fooled by the perpetual tag, these strawberries bear fruit until autumn frosts and in irregular flushes, not consistently. The type of strawberry you choose will dictate when you plant your bed. Summer fruiting varieties planted in late summer will give a good crop the following year. Any later and strictly speaking the flowers should be removed in the first summer to allow the plants to really get well established. Perpetual varieties can be planted in summer, autumn or spring.

approximate yield

Dependant on cultivar, around 750 g (1½ lb) per plant.

fruitful years

3–4 years.

cultivars

Summer

'Rosie' This is an exceptionally early variety which produces an abundance of small fruits.
'Honeoye' A reliable early cultivar with firm, very dark, shiny fruits. Has some resistance to botrytis.
'Cambridge Favourite' These strawberries are well flavoured, but perhaps not as good as others. However in its favour it is an extremely bountiful plant, which is incredibly reliable. Good disease resistance. Fruits mid-season.
'Hapil' Dependably delivers a good crop of light orange-red berries which have an intense flavour. Especially suited to light or drier soils. Mid-season
'Florence' A staggeringly prolific late cultivar with rich red fruits. Very good disease resistance.

Perpetual

'Aromel' The large berries this cultivar produces taste delightful. It may not be as productive as some, but the tasty fruit it delivers earns it a place in the garden.
'Flamenco' Consistently produces a good number of perfectly-shaped, conical strawberries. This plant starts fruiting in midsummer and will continue well into the autumn. It has excellent disease resistance.
'Viva Rosa' As well as possessing sweet pink flowers that make this decorative cultivar good value, when grown in hanging baskets or window boxes it will fruit right up to the first frost.

spacing

Arrange strawberry plants 30–38 cm (12–15 in) apart in rows. If you are planting your strawberries in a block arrange the plants in staggered rows.

planting

It is most important that the crown of the strawberry plant is not left below the soil when planting, as the plant will rot. The crown is the centre of the plant where the roots meet the foliage. Equally important is that the plant is not left high and dry with the roots exposed. The crown should sit just level with the surface of the soil. If you are planting runners you will have a small number of leaves and some long roots. Sometimes it is impossible to dig a hole large enough to spread the roots out. In this situation it is perfectly alright to trim the roots to about 10 cm (4 in) long if needed. Firm the plants in well and gently water in the plants.

Left *Remove strawberries carefully to avoid damaging the fruit or plant.*

Right *Expect strawberry plants purchased via mailorder to arrive well-wrapped for protection.*

strawberry

soil and situation

Strawberries will taste their sweetest and most delicious when grown where they can benefit from plenty of sunshine. They do best in a fertile loam, but the most important consideration is ensuring the soil is free draining. Strawberries are prone to many diseases, many of which are more prevalent if the soil is waterlogged.

maintenance

If you are not growing strawberries through sheet mulch then, once the fruits are forming, mulch around the plants with straw to keep fruit from sitting on the soil. Fresh shining straw is a great-looking mulch and strawberries look wonderful nestled in a snug bed of straw, but it does get blown all over the garden, it doesn't suppress weeds as effectively as a sheet mulch and weeding the strawberry bed is a tricky and time consuming task, so with regret I recommend planting through a strong weed suppressing membrane.

Runners (these are long stalks with tiny plantlets at the end) can be removed as they develop, unless you need more plant in which case this is one of the easiest forms of propagation. Just pot rooted runners into small pots of compost and keep well watered. Don't use runners from plants that are ailing or old, as they are probably virus ridden.

pruning

Tidy plants up in the spring, cut off any dead growth.

when to harvest

Pick strawberries as soon as their colour is fully developed. They do not keep well and are best eaten as soon as possible after picking. They can be frozen but the results are not good. What goes into the freezer as a fabulous glossy berry comes out as a soggy, discoloured daub, fit only to be hidden in things like summer puddings. Obviously strawberries make great jam.

problems and solutions

Strawberry viruses Growing cultivars with good disease resistance and buying plants from a good supplier with certified virus-free stock are the best ways to minimise the risk posed by viruses. Aphids can spread these viruses so keeping the aphid population under control will also help. Plants affected by one of these viruses will look poor, with stunted growth and yellowing or yellow blotched leaves and very little flower or fruit. The only solution is to remove the plants and destroy them, planting again in a different part of the garden. Runners from infected plants will also be infected.

Botrytis Also known as grey mould, this fungus manifests its self as a grey, fluffy growth on the fruit and leaves may turn yellow and die (see page 205).

Verticillium wilt This fungal infection can affect many trees and bushes and they may live several years. Strawberries, however, are likely to succumb almost immediately. The foliage wilts and there is nothing to be done except remove the plants swiftly and the soil around the roots, remembering not to replant strawberries in the same bed.

alpine strawberry

These are genuine 'plant them and leave them' fruits. The tough plants produce dainty, miniature strawberries with an intense and delicious flavour. These plants will literally grow anywhere – in the shade, under other plants or tucked into any corner. If you have an odd corner that needs filling then it is worth putting a few in. The plants are really quite pretty, studded with white flowers and ruby red fruits, and have a cottage garden appeal. Planted at 30 cm (12 in) intervals, they make a good edging plant for beds or paths in any part of the garden and do well in pots, window boxes or hanging baskets.

The fruits are fiddly to pick and filling a basket with any great number will take time, but they make an excellent decoration, can be used with other fruits to make puddings and can be used in summery drinks where they float like jewels. When fully ripe and deep red they are like little strawberry sweets, sugary and aromatic, so it is not surprising that children love them.

Above *The tiny alpine strawberry is packed with flavour and absolutely fool proof.*

Left *Strawberry plants are grown from runners (small plantlets). Order them from a reputable nursery to ensure good disease free plants and they will arrive in an unpromising looking bundle. Unwrap them and soak the roots in water for an hour or so then they are ready to plant.*

spacing and planting

How you space your plants will depend on the type of bed you have. In a low bed of fertile soil place plants 45 cm (17¾ in) apart with 90 cm (36 in) between rows. In a raised bed of rich soil they can successfully grown more intensively with just 30 cm (12 in) between plants and 60–75 cm (24–30 in) between rows, staggering the plants to make the most of the space and resources. I have successfully grown a block of plants just 30 cm (12 in) apart in staggered rows about 35–45 cm (14–17¾ in) apart. This is very intensive growing and needs very good conditions to work.

creating a low-maintenance strawberry bed

A bed of summer fruiting varieties will go on earning its keep for three or four years, so it is worth setting it up well. Chose an early, mid season and late fruiting summer variety and you will still have a long harvest period, and creating a strawberry bed is a more worthwhile project.

Incorporating a seep hose in the bed and planting through a weed suppressing membrane makes the strawberry bed incredibly easy to maintain. No weeding for three or four years and watering is as easy as connecting up a hose – two simple measures that ensure great productivity.

Ideally, prepare the bed in summer. Choose a sunny, sheltered spot for your strawberry bed, though the plants will tolerate a small amount of shade. If you are planning a low bed, dig in plenty of well-rotted manure. If you are using a new raised bed use the deep bed mulch method (see pages 34–35) to fill the bed and end with a layer of top soil, or fill the bed with a 50/50 mix of topsoil and well-rotted organic matter.

1 Lay a length of seep hose on the soil, arranging it such that the whole bed will be irrigated. Leave the hose connection drooping over the end of the bed. The pipes are easier to manipulate when warm, so leave it in the sun or soak it in warm water.

2 Cover the soil and hose with a sheet of woven weed suppressing membrane, pulling it as taught as possible. This will keep the soil warm, prevent weeds from growing and keep the fruits clean, so it is well worth including. The membrane should last for the life of the bed and can be reused.

3 Cut cross shaped slits in the membrane and plant the runners through the resulting hole. Plant them so the crown of the plant (the crown is where the roots meet the plant) is level with the soil surface. Any deeper and the plant may rot. If you hit the irrigation pipe ease it to one side. This is fiddly but you are saving three or four years weeding.

Above *Just a few weeks on and already the runners are well established.*

tree fruit

The hardest part of growing a fruit tree is planning where to position it before the tree is either bought or planted. Choosing the right variety, on the right rootstock, for the right location needs careful thought as that tree will hopefully be with you for at least 30 years, and some will quite possibly still be growing where you plant them in over a hundred years time. Obviously trees can be removed if they become a nuisance, but that is always a shame. Better to put some thought into the location and choice of tree at the outset.

In general, trees like a sunny open location. They will not thrive planted under the canopy of other trees or too close to other trees, which will compete for nutrients, water and light. Imagine the impact the new tree will have in a few years time – will it be blocking a pleasant view, shading out other plants or seating areas? So when you choose the tree think about which rootstock (see page 101) it should be on, as the rootstock governs how tall the tree might grow. The eventual height of the tree will also influence how easy it is to maintain and its fruit is to harvest. Even in the smallest of gardens tree fruits can be grown as ballerina trees, which grow as a single stem with no side branches. This form requires no pruning at all and can be grown in open ground or in pots. Trees often described as 'patio trees' are grafted onto a very dwarfing rootstock and will grow happily in a pot on the terrace, though they can be planted in open ground where they will need much less attention.

Choosing the type of fruit tree to grow should not be hard. Apples or pears? Plums or cherries? You will know what you like and most tree fruit will do well in any open site in reasonable soil, but choosing the exact variety may be more difficult. Open any good nursery catalogue and there will be tens or even hundreds of excellent varieties you will not have tasted or possibly even heard of. The descriptions in a good catalogue are helpful but so are tasting events often held by large nurseries, gardens and fruit growers. Peaches, nectarines and apricots will only thrive in warmer areas.

To guarantee the best chances of success it is worth investing in well developed trees from a good supplier so you can be confident they are free of pests and diseases and have received the best care possible before they reach you (they have been lifted correctly, for example, if they are bareroot). When choosing a tree it is tempting to plump for the tallest, but look for a good open framework of stout branches that should develop into a nicely shaped tree.

the basics

- Trees will be part of the garden for a long time, so consider their eventual height and spread carefully when choosing where to plant them.
- Only grow varieties you like to eat.
- Buy three-year-old trees from a good nursery so the skill and hard work of establishing a good framework of branches has been done for you.
- If you want to keep things easy do not opt for fan trained, espalier or other restricted tree forms. Good, well-timed pruning twice a year is vital to keep the trees in shape and fruitful.
- Choose ballerina trees if you are very short of space, or grow ballerina or patio trees in containers.

Left *Growing fruit trees on dwarfing rootstocks means the fruit is more easily harvested.*

tree shapes

Fruit trees can be pruned, bent and cajoled into many miraculous shapes that are normally far removed from the shape a tree would naturally take and, as you might expect, when you take on nature it is a battle. Keeping trained trees in the desired shape is hard work, requiring very careful, timely pruning and a foresight far greater than general pruning. The forms are essentially decorative and the pruning is a combination of the need to regulate growth as well as encourage fruitfulness. Errors here can be disastrous and costly. Fan training against a wall is useful for tender, warmth-loving fruit and minarets are a great space-saving option and may be worth considering if you want to learn the pruning skills and have time to religiously apply them. Otherwise, for an easy life, avoid beautifully trained trees.

standard trees

- Up to 9 m (30 ft) tall.
- About a 2 m (6½ ft) trunk.
- Up to 6 m (20 ft) between trees.
- Only remedial pruning (removing dead wood and crossing branches).
- Difficult to harvest fruit and impossible to net.
- Suitable apple rootstocks: MM111, M25.

half standard

- Up to 6 m (20 ft) tall.
- 60–90 cm (24–36 in) trunk.
- Only remedial pruning.
- Difficult to harvest fruit and net.
- Suitable apple rootstocks: MM106, M25; pears on quince A; peaches, plums, gages, damsons and nectarines Saint Julian A or Torinel; cherry on colt.

bush

- Up to 6 m (20 ft). Can be as short as 1.8 m (6 ft) on M27.
- 60–75 cm (24–29½ in) trunk.
- Suitable root stocks: apple M27, M9, M26, MM106; pears Quince A or Quince C; plums, gages and damsons on pixy; peaches, nectarines, damsons, apricots, plums and gages on Saint Julian A or Torinel; cherry on Gisela 5 or colt.

ballerina

- A compact column space saving tree.
- Grows to 2.5 m (8 ft) with no side branches.
- No pruning required.

Bought as three-year-old trees with a good established framework the above freestanding tree forms are straightforward to prune, the ballerina tree is the easiest to manage. It requires absolutely no pruning at all, and it is very easy to net and pick the fruit, but the yield will obviously be limited. Other space-saving trees are less straightforward to prune and require support. Their restricted shapes take years of skilled pruning and planning to achieve and is not easy to achieve and so creating fan trained, espalier and step-over trees falls outside the scope of this book.

It is possible to buy well-trained fan trained trees or espalier trees, and this is the route I would recommend to the novice if they had set their heart on having a trained tree in the garden. However, because of the age of the trees and the work that has gone into their creation they are expensive. Once formed, the shapes have to be carefully and accurately pruned to maintain the framework. As well as rendering unproductive walls and fences fruitful these trained forms look fantastic when mature and well kept, but they are really not for the time poor, slapdash, erratic gardener or those who just want tasty fruit for the minimum of effort.

cordon

- A single stem usually grown at 45 degrees to the ground against wires on a wall or freestanding.
- Height about 1.8 m (6 ft), spread 75 cm (29½ in).
- Allows several trees to be planted in small space.

espalier

- Height 2.5 m (8 ft), spread up to 4.5 m (15 ft).
- Branches are trained out horizontally at about 30 cm (12 in) intervals from a vertical trunk.
- Used for apples and pears.

fan

- Used for cherries, plums, peaches, nectarines and apricots.
- Grow to about 2.5 m (8 ft) high and 3.5 m (12 ft) wide.
- Formed from a short trunk with two branches from which others radiate.
- Very careful pruning required.
- Arguably the prettiest tree form.

step-over

- Grown to about 30 cm (12 in) high.
- A short trunk with two horizontal branches.
- Used for edging paths and beds.
- Very ornamental but not much of a harvest for the input needed.

rootstock

Fruit trees are generally grown grafted onto a rootstock other than their own. This allows trees to be grown in smaller spaces than if they were grown on their own roots, as the rootstocks influence how the fruit tree grows. They control how quickly a tree grows, how vigorous it is, its ultimate size, when it will start fruiting, and even the quality of the fruit. The graft can be seen on most trees, a knobbly lump just above ground level where the tree and the rootstock have been joined or grafted together. It is important that this graft stays well above soil level and any shoot growing directly from the roots, known as suckers, are cut off below soil level. Occasionally the graft is made where the trunk meets the crown of the tree.

The major influence of the rootstock is on the size of the tree. Each rootstock will ultimately produce a different size of tree suited to being grown as a particular form. Choosing a dwarfing rootstock not only means fruit can be picked and trees pruned more easily, trees on a dwarfing rootstock have the advantage of producing fruit earlier. Very dwarfing rootstocks even allow otherwise towering trees to be grown in patio containers.

It is worth remembering that the rootstock is only part of the story when it comes to determining tree growth – the growing conditions and variety are the other. On a very dwarfing rootstock trees need good conditions to give their best and even then the harvest will be low. Or looking at it another way, if you propose to grow trees in poor soil a more vigorous rootstock might be needed to get a reasonable sized, productive tree. Reputable suppliers should always be able to tell you which rootstock a tree is growing on, or at least the predicted height and spread of the tree. Specialist nurseries will usually have each variety grafted onto a choice of rootstocks.

Trees should always be planted at the same level they have been growing in the pot. Special attention should be paid to ensure the graft is above soil level.

rootstock

apples

M27

- Extremely dwarfing.
- 1.2–1.8 m (4–6 ft) tall.
- Suitable for container grown trees and cordons.
- Require a fertile soil, will need watering in periods of drought.
- Area around the tree must be kept clear of competing vegetation.
- Need permanent staking.
- First fruit after 2 years.

M9

- Very dwarfing.
- 1.8–3 m (6–10 ft) tall.
- Suited to small gardens and bush trees.
- Require good soil and irrigation in dry periods.
- Area around the tree must be kept clear of competing vegetation.
- Requires permanent staking.
- First fruit at 2 or 3 years.

M26

- Dwarfing.
- 2.5–3 m (8–10 ft) tall.
- Small garden tree in any soil.
- Permanent staking.
- First fruit after 2 or 3 years.

MM106

- Semi-dwarfing.
- Most popular apple rootstock.
- 3.5–5.5 m (12–18 ft) tall.
- Suited to all tree forms but not a good choice in a small garden.
- Any soil, including poor soils.
- Stake until 5 years old.
- Fruits in 3 to 4 years

M25

- Vigorous.
- 4.5–5.5 m (1 –18 ft) tall.
- Standard and half standard trees used in orchards, too large for most gardens.
- Any soil, including poor soils.
- Stake for three years.
- Fruits in 5 to 6 years.

MM111 and M2

- Vigorous.
- 5.5–6.5 m (18–22 ft) tall.
- Too large for most gardens.
- Any soil.
- Stake for three years.
- Fruits in 4 or 5 years.

pears

Quince A

- Medium vigour.
- 3–6 m (10–20 ft) tall.
- Used for most pears.
- Stake for 5 years.
- First fruit in 4 years.

Quince C

- Moderately vigorous.
- 2.2–4.5 m (8–18 ft) tall.
- Not good in poor conditions.
- Fruits in 4 to 7 years.

Pear stock

- Very vigorous.
- Large standard trees.
- Not suited to average gardens.

cherries

Gisela 5

- Dwarfing.
- Suited to bush and restricted forms.
- 1.8–2.75 m (6–9 ft) tall.
- Easier to net and pick fruit than larger forms.
- Needs a fertile soil.
- Stake permanently.
- First fruit in 3 to 4 years.

Colt

- Semi vigorous.
- Suited to standard, half standard and bush forms
- 4.5–5.5 m (15–18 ft) tall.
- Any soil.
- Stake permanently.
- First fruit in 3 to 4 years.

plums, gages and damsons

Pixy

- Moderately dwarfing.
- Suitable for dwarf bush trees.
- 3–3.5 m (10–12 ft) tall.
- Requires a good soil.
- Permanent stake required.
- Fruits in 3 to 4 years.

plums, gages, damsons, peaches and nectarines

Saint Julian A

- Moderately vigorous.
- Suitable for bush or half standard trees.
- 4.25–5 m (14–18 ft) tall.
- Stake for 5 years.
- First fruit in 3 to 4 years.

Above *A slight lump on the trunk of the tree shows the point at which the grafted material joins the rootstock.*

apple

Not perhaps the most glamorous of fruit, but an incredibly useful and versatile staple. The trees are not really eye catching for most of the year, but the apple tree in full bloom is simply beautiful and sometimes self-fertile. There are such a diverse range of apple cultivars that there is something to appeal to all tastes, from the sharp and crisp, to the aromatic and almost spicy Cox, to the soft and mealy. There are literally thousands (I recently read 7000+) different apples in cultivation representing hundreds of years of hard work by nursery men and some lucky finds. Those on offer at the supermarket are just a small handful. The catalogue of any specialist nursery will have a mind boggling list of apples, some with the most arresting names like 'Slack ma Girdle', 'Cornish Giliflower' and 'Foxwhelp'.

There are dessert apples, cider apples, cultivars for cooking, crab apples and those that will do a reasonable job as a dessert and cooking apple. In fact, if you only have room for one fruit tree choosing a dual purpose cultivar makes sense. It is even possible to grow several types of apple on one tree. These are known as family trees, where two or three cultivars are grafted onto one rootstock. Good catalogues will have a description of the character of the apples, but as your tree will be with you for some time, it will in all probability outlive you, it is worth tasting a few unfamiliar varieties if you can before selecting your trees. Nurseries and large orchards often have open days in the autumn to celebrate the harvest and introduce people to the range of trees on offer.

Once you have sorted out the varieties that appeal to you need to choose a rootstock which will give you the right sized tree for your space. The only remaining task is to ensure your apple blossom will be pollinated efficiently and bear fruit. Not all apples are self-fertile; they need another apple to pollinate them, some need two. This is usually not a concern, if you live in an area with a reasonable number of fruit trees the odds are you need not worry. If you are in an area devoid of apple trees and growing just one tree choose a self-fertile variety. To make life easier apples are divided into pollination groups, so it is easy to work out which trees will successfully pollinate each other. Put simply, apples that blossom a similar time will pollinate each other. Good nursery catalogues and garden centre labels will show a cultivars pollination group.

when will tree bear fruit

3–4 years depending on variety on dwarfing or semi-dwarfing rootstock.

approximate yield

20 kg (44 lb) for dwarf bush, 27–45 kg (60–100 lb) for bush, 90–180 kg (200–400 lb) for a mature standard.

fruitful years

Can be hundreds but the most productive years are likely to be 10–40.

Left *Cox-style 'Laxon's Superb' tolerates cold winters, has an excellent flavour and ripens late in the season.*

pollination groups

These are usually denoted by the letters A to F or number 1 to 6. Trees in one group will pollinate those in the same group and the groups either side. So, trees in group C are successfully pollinated by trees in groups C, B and D. No suitable pollinator means no apples!

If all this seems like too much hard work, plant a crab apple tree such as 'John Downie'. They are very attractive and produce so much pollen over a long period they should take care of all your apple trees. Traditionally orchards were furnished with one crab to 30 to 40 trees to guarantee a good crop.

apple

cultivars

Cookers

'Bramley's Seedling' Dating from 1806, this is an incredibly popular cooking apple. The fruit is large and pale green. The trees are very large and will easily engulf a small garden. They tend produce a fantastic crop one year and much fewer apples the next, and this is often described as biennial bearing. Pollination group D (needs two pollinators).

'Reverend W Wilks' This cultivar has three great advantages; good disease resistance, being reliably self-fertile and a neat compact habit. The fruits are pale green with a pinkish blush and produced in great volume. There is always a 'but' and in this case, like the Bramley, it is a biennial bearer. Pollination group B.

'Annie Elizabeth' A fantastic choice for anyone who intends to store their apples. These apples should be good right through to the end of the following spring. Pollination group C.

Dual-purpose apples

'James Grieve' On the positive side, this cultivar is partially self fertile, prolific, very early and hardy. However it can be prone to canker and the bumper crop it reliably delivers does not keep well. Pollination group B.

'Blenheim Orange' An amazingly old variety, probably dating from 1740, which is still a great favourite as it produces a massive crop of exceptional apples and has good mildew resistance. It is a vigorous tree and can be slow to start cropping. A good choice for cold areas. Pollination group B (requires two pollinators).

Eating apples

'Ashmead's Kernel' At just a little over 300 years old, this excellently flavoursome apple is justifiably a great favourite. Yields may not be as hefty as some but the fruit is fantastic, keeps well and a reasonable tree will produce more than enough to justify its place in the garden. Pollination group C.

'Sunset' This is great tree for those who love the taste of the Cox but don't want to put up with its uppity behaviour (the Cox demands nearly perfect growing conditions to do well, is suseptable to frost damage and is prone to go down with every disease going). Sunset is compact, easy going, reliably self-fertile and provides a weighty harvest. Pollination group B.

'Egremont Russet' I always imagine the russet as a type of fruit in its own right, as these apples are quite unlike any other. Their rough, brown skins, the texture of their flesh and distinctive, aromatic taste sets them apart. The fruits are small but there are plenty of them. Not a good keeper. Pollination group B (partially self fertile).

'Discovery' Bright red, smallish apples that really appeal to children. The trees have a tidy habit and are a good choice for smaller gardens. It has good disease resistance and will put up with frost. Pollination group B.

'Katy' One of the best for cold regions, producing an immense crop year after year. Pollination group B.

For a list of the best apples for keeping, see page 209.

spacing

Top left *An unfussy, self-fertile tree, 'Green Sleeves' is a good choice if you only have a spot for one dessert apple.*

Right *The blossom of 'Laxton's Superb' is fairly resistant to frost and the russeted red apples should keep into late winter.*

apple

Allow 3.5–5.5 m (12–18 ft) between bush trees, 2.5–4.5 m (8–15 ft) between dwarf bush trees, and 5.5–12 m (18–30 ft) for a standard.

planting

Plant bareroot trees during the dormant period when the ground is not frozen. Planting as soon after leaf fall as possible gives the trees the best possible start. All trees on dwarfing rootstocks require a stout stake to support them as long as they live as the root systems are not beefy enough to support the tree. Others need staking for the first five years or so unless your trees are in a particularly exposed location. Young trees do better if they have a 1 m (3 ft) diameter circle around their trunk kept clear of all vegetation, and well covered in a mulch of garden compost for the first two or three years. Trees on dwarfing rootstocks need this clear area maintained throughout their life as they are not suited to dealing with competition.

soil and situation

Ideally plant your apple trees in a fairly sheltered spot in reasonable soil.

maintenance

Water newly planted trees until they find their feet. Trees on very dwarfing rootstocks, especially those in containers, will require more care than larger trees, as more care is needed with watering and feeding. Larger trees in open ground should just about look after themselves except in periods of severe drought. In the spring feed with a multi-purpose organic fertilizer and mulch an area about 1 m (3 ft) in diameter with good organic matter.

pruning

Prune in winter. If you plant a tree with the formative pruning done for you, growing on a modern restricting rootstock, all that needs to be done is to remove any diseased or damaged wood as well as 'water shoots' (long, whippy growth that comes directly from the trunk) and crossing or inconveniently placed branches. Be decisive and cut branches to be removed right back to just outside the collar (where they meet the next branch or the trunk). Overzealous pruning, or just removing all the outer growth, can result in strong re-growth which is not fruit-bearing.

Left *Very much like a Cox but much easier to grow, 'Fiesta' has the same aromatic flavour and produces plenty of apples.*

when to harvest

Ripe apples should come away from the tree with just a gentle twist. Harvesting too soon can require some strong tugging which can damage the tree, as the twiggy growth and small branches tend to be quite brittle and come away with the unripe fruit. Many apples will be fine left on the tree for a while until you are ready to pick them. Keep an eye on the weather though, as high winds will see your crop knocked to the ground, bruise and be unfit for keeping.

problems and solutions

Trees losing young formed fruit As a natural part of the tree's fruit producing cycle, a proportion of the young fruit simply fall from the tree. Some years it is more pronounced than others.

Split fruit The most likely cause of split fruit is an erratic water supply.

Fireblight As the name suggests, the young growth of the tree dies back and becomes brown, looking as if it has been burned. Cankers, wounds that ooze in the spring, form in the diseases tissue. There is no treatment beyond cutting back all of the branches showing signs of disease by 60 cm (24 in) into healthy wood and sealing the wound. Destroy the material you remove and sterilize your secateurs and pruning saw.

Woolly aphid These aphids look like a small wodge of cotton wool crammed into the crevices of the apple tree's bark. They suck sap from the tree. They do little direct damage, however they open up wounds in the tree bark, which can allow in diseases. They can be removed with a stiff brush.

Codling moth, mildew, canker and scab See pages 203–205.

pear

Pears are, perhaps surprisingly, just a little fussy. If the conditions are right they will thrive, but they are far harder to please than apples and don't keep as well. They flower earlier so are more prone to frost damage, require more warmth and sun to produce a good crop and need sheltering from strong winds. However, if you are a pear lover and have the right situation, they will furnish you with a good crop with minimum care.

Like apples, most pears require another pear flowering at about the same time to pollinate its flowers, and some require two other cultivars. Pears are split into four pollination groups and will pollinate cultivars in the same group and those from adjacent groups. If you have room for only one pear, grow 'Conference'. It will produce some fruits without cross-pollination (though yields are higher with a pollinator) and is generally less fussy than most.

when will tree bear fruit

5–6 years.

approximate yield

Bush, 18–45 kg (40–100 lb); dwarf bush, 9–18 kg (20–40 lb); standard, 36–109 kg (80–240 lb).

fruitful years

40–100+ years.

cultivars

'Beth' A tasty, slightly irregular pear that would probably be rejected by most supermarkets, but the fruits are sweet and juicy and ideally sized for children. The tree is a real star in being both hardy and reliable. Pollination group B.

'Beurre Hardy' This amazingly flavoursome pear is yellowish-green in colour. Unfortunately the tree is probably a little large for smaller plots and is slow to begin fruiting. Pollination group B.

'Conference' My favourite, especially when they are under-ripe and home-grown. I am not alone – good yields, reasonable hardiness, the ability to fruit without a pollinator and willingness to fruit in less than perfect conditions makes it a popular choice. The fruits are a green with brown russet skins and elongated. Pollination group B.

'Williams' Bon Chetien' This is an old variety dating from 1770 producing stout, plump, yellow fruit. I mention it as it scores highly for its hardiness, but unfortunately is prone to scab and doesn't store well. Pollination group B.

planting and spacing

Plant bareroot trees in the dormant season as soon after leaf fall as possible, while the soil is still warm. This is rather more important with pears than other tress as they start to grow early in the year, so when

Top left *Pear 'Beurre d'Aremberg'.*

Right *'Gorham' is a green, russeted pear with a good flavour. The trees reliably deliver a good harvest.*

Above *Unlike apples, pears are picked under-ripe and should come away from the tree with a slight twist.*

pear

apple trees are still in their winter slumbers and can be safely planted, the pear tree will be waking. Container grown trees can be planted at any time but will do best and be less of a burden if planted in late autumn. The tree will require staking.

soil and situation

Pears really do need warmth and shelter as the blossom and young growth is easily damaged by frosts and cold winds. Planting in the snug microclimate generated by a wall or fence may help. If your location is less than ideal make life easy by growing 'Conference' or 'Beth'. Pears will tolerate heavy soils but not thin, poor or dry chalky soils. The ideal is a fertile, well-drained but moisture retentive soil.

pruning and maintenance

The care a pear needs is much the same as the apple (see page 109).

when to harvest

Pears are difficult to harvest, or rather knowing exactly when to harvest them is difficult. Unlike apples, they should not be left on the tree to ripen but picked just before they are ripe and stored until ready to eat (see pages 208–209), which is a bit of a nuisance. With apples you might stroll out, pick a bowlful for the house and safely leave the rest. Not so for pears. If you wish to enjoy them at their very best the pears have to be picked while they are still firm but sweet-tasting. Too soon and they will not ripen, too late and they will rot. Even though they are not fully ripe they should still part from the tree with just a slight twist of the wrist – no branch-breaking tugging required.

problems and solutions

Thankfully pears are less prone to problems than some fruit trees. The most likely cause of problems will be less than ideal growing conditions; these might manifest themselves in few fruit, stunted fruit and a less than vibrant looking tree. Scab (see page 203) and fireblight may be a problem.

sweet and sour cherries

Home-grown cherries, left on the tree until they are perfectly ripe and glossy, develop a sweetness and concentration of flavour that is unlikely to be had in those found in the shops. They are one of the most luxurious tasting fruits you can grow in your plot. If you want to enjoy the indulgence of basketfuls of cherries, however, you have to be prepared to do battle with the bird population – along with blueberries and redcurrants, cherries are a real favourite. Even the sour culinary cherry trees will be stripped. Trees should be netted as soon as the fruit begins to form – wait too long and the fruit will be gone.

The sheer luxury of the cherry is amplified by a very short season. Most sweet cherry varieties ripen within four weeks or so of each other, and all the fruit on a tree will ripen more or less in one hit, though some newer varieties stretch the harvest period. The pollination requirements of cherry trees are complex. Self-infertile trees require another tree to be in flower at the same time, and it has to be the right tree! Many cherry trees are incompatible. The easy option is to grow modern, self-fertile varieties.

Right *The delicate white blossom of the morello cherry.*

when will tree bear fruit

3 years patio trees on Gisela 3 rootstock; 4–5 years on semi dwarfing, colt rootstock; 5–6 years standard trees.

approximate yield

Half-standard, standard and bush 13½–54½ kg (30–120 lb). Patio container-grown trees much less.

fruitful years

50+ years. These are long-lived trees but fruitfulness will decline.

cultivars

'Stella' Dark red fruit on a vigorous, trouble-free tree. Self-fertile, sweet cherry.

'Sunburst' Wonderfully flavoured fruit, so dark it is almost black. Strong growing tree. Self-fertile sweet cherry.

'Lapins Cherokee' Dark red fruits with an excellent flavour. This cultivar does seem to drop a large number of fruitlets, but this is nothing to worry about. Self-fertile, sweet cherry.

'Sweet heart' Deep, black, gorgeously glossy cherries produced on a well behaved tree. This modern cultivar is popular because, unlike most other cherry trees, the

Left *Irresistible 'Stella', a reliable, self-fertile cherry that will cope in northern areas.*

Right *Yet to fully ripen, these sour cherries are used only in cooking and preserves.*

sweet and sour cherries

fruit ripens over a period of a few weeks, so rather than having a glut, where some have to be frozen or used for preserves, you can enjoy more of the fabulous fruit straight from the tree. Self-fertile sweet cherry.
'Morello' This is the most well-known of the sour cherries. The fruits are dark red and can be used in pies and preserves. The 'Morello' will grow in shady locations and is often recommended for clothing north-facing walls. Self-fertile, sour cherry.

spacing

A bush tree should be 3 m (10 ft) from its neighbour. If you try a fan trained tree allow it 3.5 m (12 ft) to spread its branches across.

planting

Bareroot cherry trees will usually establish better than container grown plants. Both are best planted in the dormant season so long as the ground is not frozen.

soil and situation

Cherry trees do not enjoy having wet feet; they require a well drained soil to thrive. In fact if the soil is too damp they will die. If you have any doubts, dig a test hole a couple of feet deep where you plan to plant the trees and watch how long rain water sits in the hole. This aside, they will tolerate a range of soils, but a fertile loam is best.

maintenance

Mulch around young trees and feed with a general purpose organic fertilizer in the early spring. Protecting your crop from the birds is essential. Net the trees early or the birds will get there before you.

pruning

Buy well formed trees at three years old with a good basic framework and then leave them alone as far as you can. Any pruning, even that done in the summer, risks sparking off a silver leaf attack.

when to harvest

For the best sweetness and delicious flavours leave the cherries hanging from the trees until they are completely ripe. They are best enjoyed almost immediately. They can be kept for just a few days in the refrigerator. Cherries can be tray frozen once the stone has been removed and made into preserves.

problems and solutions

Silver leaf The symptoms of silver leaf are reasonably easy to spot – as the name suggests a number of leaves take on a silvery appearance (see page 205).
Birds There is no point growing cherries unless you protect them with netting well before the fruit is ripe. If you don't do this you will be extremely lucky to taste a single ripe cherry. You may think you are getting away with not protecting the tree if the fruits start to colour and remain untouched, then at some imperceptible signal the birds set to work and within the day the majority will probably be gone.
Canker, brown rot and aphids See pages 203–205.

plum

There are so many cultivars of plum to choose from that you could be picking plums from midsummer through to the autumn. A good plum with a tender skin and fresh, sweet flesh is a marvellous dessert fruit. However you will have to be prepared to give away or process some of your hefty crop. Plums do not keep unless picked under-ripe, and even then they will only keep for two or three weeks in a cool place. So once your tree is established you could be faced with a large harvest to deal with – up to 27 kg (60 lb) for a bush tree and a whopping 54½ kg (120 lb) for a standard. Inevitably some of the crop is lost to birds, wasps or other problems, but the fantastic productivity of the trees guarantees a good crop for the gardener. Plums can be made into preserves or wine and can be frozen if they are first cut in half and tray frozen before putting into bags. As with some apples and pears, certain plums require pollination by a different cultivar that flowers at the same time. Plums are split into three pollination groups: A, B and C. Plums in each group will pollinate those in the same group or the ones next to it. If early flowering cultivars, that is those in group A, do not have their flowers damaged by the frost then there is the equally troublesome fact that pollinating insect are in short supply at that time of year, so few fruit may set. It is easier to stick to one of the many later flowering cultivars for a better chance of a great crop.

Right *The 'Victoria' plum has flavoursome, yellow flesh and is wonderfully sweet when properly ripe.*

when will tree bear fruit

5 years, slightly earlier on very dwarfing pixy root stock.

approximate yield

13½–45 kg (30–100 lb).

fruitful years

Tens of years on dwarfing rootstock, perhaps hundreds when grown as a standard.

cultivars

'Victoria' Quite rightly a great garden favourite. It has beautifully flavoured firm, yellow flesh, and produces a prodigious amount of fruit which ripen in late summer. The plums cook well. This is a self-fertile cultivar so if you want just one plum tree this is an excellent choice. It does have two faults: firstly, it tends to fruit biennially if fruits are not thinned, that means it produces a great crop one year and next to nothing the next as it recuperates from the effort; and secondly it is susceptible to silver leaf disease. Compatibilty group C.

'Marjorie's Seedling' This is a later, purple-skinned plum which fruits in early to mid autumn. Cooks well and is self-fertile. Compatibility group C.

'Czar' This culinary cultivar is an ideal choice for colder regions as has frost-resistant flowers. The plums are acidic and classed as a culinary plum, but when fully ripe they are edible straight from the tree if you like your fruit a little sharp. Self-fertile and fruits in late summer. Compatibility Group C.

'President' Introduced in 1901, this dual-purpose cultivar produces a prodigious amount of large, dark purple, bloom-covered fruit. It is one of the latest plums to ripen, and is beautifully sweet when left on the tree to fully ripen but is also excellent for cooking. Compatibility Group C.

spacing

Space all tree forms on St Julien 3.5–4.5 m (12–15 ft) apart, bush trees on pixy 3–3.5 m (10–12 ft) apart.

planting

Plant bareroot trees in the dormant period. Container grown trees can be planted at any time, but for an easy life, plant container grown trees in the autumn. Young trees will need staking.

soil and situation

Plums tend to flower early and the blossom can easily be damaged by frosts. Frost damage is probably the

plum

most common cause of irregular cropping in plum trees. To avoid this problem, choose a late flowering cultivar and plant it in the warmest spot in the garden. In cold areas grow against a south facing wall and then the blossom can easily be protected with netting if frosts are forecast. Plums like good, deep, moisture-retentive soils.

maintenance

Protect blossom from frost if you can. Flinging horticultural fleece, hessian or even old net curtains over small trees should do the trick, and container grown plants are easily cosseted. Unfortunately with larger trees this is unlikely to be possible.

Plums are so very prolific, it may be necessary to support laden branches as they bow down. If trees are carrying an abundance of fruitlets (young fruits), it is worth removing some of the crop. Plum branches are reasonably brittle and the weight of a heavy crop will break them. This is not just a shame because it damages the tree, but also because the open wound it creates is likely to allow in silver leaf or canker.

Mulch around the tree annually and apply a general purpose fertilizer in accordance with the manufacturers instructions in early spring.

pruning

Once the basic framework has been formed at three years the trees are best left alone as pruning gives silver leaf the opportunity to enter the wounds. Any dead or damaged wood can be taken out in the spring or summer.

when to harvest

Plums on the same tree ripen at more or less the same time but not at exactly the same time, so the complete harvest will take three or four attempts. Plums taste best and sweetest if left on the tree to completely ripen and so keep poorly once picked. Pick fruits slightly firmer for preserve making. Plums can be stoned and frozen.

problems and solutions

Silver leaf One of the most serious problems you are likely to come across is silver leaf (see page 203). Remove affected branches quickly, cutting 15 cm (6 in) into healthy wood, and avoid the problem by only doing minimal remedial pruning in the late spring or summer.
Brown rot and bacterial canker See pages 203–205.
Birds The birds can do a great deal of damage as they pick off flower buds in the spring and eat the fruit when it is ripe. On small trees nets or fleece can be used to keep the birds off, though if you have a large number of trees or standard trees this is really not practical and you have to rely on the tree generosity in producing copious amounts of fruit to leave some to harvest. Wasps will also happily feast on ripe fruit and can become a nuisance in the small garden as they are drawn to windfalls.

Left *Less frequently available in shops than plums, gages are worth growing for their intense flavour.*

greengage

The fruits of a gage tree are small and round and arguably have a more intense flavour than the plum. They are also much sweeter than a dessert plum. Greengages are grown in much the same way as plums, though unfortunately they are more susceptible to frost damage and crops tend to be lighter.

damson

Cultivated as plums, damson trees are extremely hardy and reliably provide a profusion of fruit in exposed areas where other fruit trees might fail. They can even be used to provide a sheltered belt alongside the exposed side of other fruit trees. The damson is not as popular as its fleshier, sweeter relative the plum, probably because it is not really a dessert fruit but rather better suited to jam making. The small fruits tend to be quite tart and sharp but with a rich, deep flavour. They are tough, rustic trees which are very easy and undemanding to grow but only really of value to the jam or wine maker. The fruit really does make fantastic, full-flavoured jam.

when will tree bear fruit

3 years on pixy rootstock, 4–5 years St Julian rootstock.

approximate yield

13½–54½ kg (30–120 lb).

fruitful years

At least 40 years.

cultivars

'Merryweather' A good all-rounder, producing largish blue-black fruits excellent for cooking and eating straight from the tree if you enjoy your fruit on the sharp side. Self-fertile.

'Shropshire' Also known as Prune Damson, ripens late in the season in early autumn. Will make a larger tree than 'Merryweather'.

soil and location

Extremely unfussy, will tolerate a windy site.

maintenance

Mulch around trees annually in early spring and apply a good general purpose organic feed.

pruning

Once the basic structure of the tree has formed at three years no pruning is required beyond removing dead wood or any showing signs of disease. This is usually best done sometime in the spring or summer to guard against infection by silver leaf.

when to harvest

As soon as the fruits are ripe and give slightly when gently squeezed.

problems and solutions

These are tough, resilient trees and seldom have any problems.

Right *Damsons are smaller than plums and lack their ample flesh and sweetness.*

peach

Peach trees are one of the prettiest fruit trees. In the spring they dazzle with pink blossom and the tree is then clothed in slender, graceful, long, willow-like leaves. The fruit is no less appealing than the tree – generous, juicy flesh with soft downy skin – 'pretty as a peach'. Peaches are not easy-going or easy to grow, especially in colder regions. A good, long, warm summer is needed to ripen the fruit. A cold winter is not a problem but as they flower early in the year there can be a shortage of pollinators and frost can damage the blossom. Heavy rains and wind are also damaging. Growing peach trees in a fan form against a south or southwest facing wall can help create the necessary microclimate, but this requires great attention to detail and sound, reliable pruning. The easier option is to grow peaches in containers on dwarfing rootstocks. This way blossom can be easily protected and the trees placed in the most favourable location at any time of year, even in a greenhouse or conservatory when they are in blossom. For all this fuss you have to really want those peaches.

when will tree bear fruit

3 years on dwarfing rootstock, 4–5 years on St Julien.

approximate yield

A bush tree could yield 13.5–22.5 kg (30–50 lb) of fruit.

fruitful years

Not long-lived.

cultivars

'Peregrine' Reliable and prolific, Peregrine produces well-flavoured, yellow-fleshed fruits that ripen in midsummer.
'Rochester' Blooming slightly later than Peregrine, this cultivar is probably the most reliable variety to grow in areas where frosts may be a problem.
'Hayles Early' Known for the profusion of fruits it bears which ripen in midsummer.
'Red Haven' Fairly robust and is resistant to peach leaf curl.

spacing

Fans on St. Julien A, 3.5 m (12 ft) apart.
Bush trees on St. Julien A, 4.5–5.5 m (15–18 ft) apart.

Left *Peach 'Bonanza'.*

planting

Plant bareroot trees in the dormant period or container grown trees at any time of year, though they are easiest to manage if planted in early autumn.

soil and situation

The key to growing peaches well is a well-drained soil. They will tolerate many soil types so long as they are free-draining. The site chosen should be the warmest, most sheltered possible.

maintenance

A generous layer of mulch applied annually in the spring helps to maintain moisture in the soil. The difficulty here is balancing the peach tree's considerable need for water and a free draining situation. Trees need adequate water or the fruit will split, but the trees will not tolerate water-logging. If you are unsure about how well the proposed site for your tree drains, dig a hole 60 cm–1 m (2–3 ft) deep and observe how quickly rain water drains away. Apply a general balanced organic fertilizer in the spring. Thinning the peach fruitlets is a good idea, this means the remaining peaches are more likely to reach a good size and the tree doesn't become weakened by producing a prodigious harvest.

peach

pruning

Prune in spring and summer. Peach trees produce fruit on young growth, so the aim of pruning is to encourage the tree to throw up plenty of new growth. The upper branches should be cut back to keep the centre open and stimulate strong new growth which will bear fruit the following year. Aim to take out about one quarter of the older wood. This is known as regenerative pruning. Any dead or unproductive wood can also be removed. A peach tree that is not pruned will still fruit, but the fruit will be held on the new wood around the edges of the tree.

when to harvest

When ripe, the fruit will easily come away from the tree when lifted slightly. Once picked, peaches only keep for a few days in a cool place. The fruits can be used in jams or frozen if first chopped and the stones removed. Lay the pieces of fruit on a tray to freeze and then transfer to airtight bags. Once defrosted the peach loses most of its glorious character, so enjoy as many fresh as you can.

problems and solutions

Peach leaf curl Peach trees are prone to peach leaf curl. This fungal disease produces large, unpleasant-looking reddish blisters on the leaves. It causes early leaf fall and can weaken the tree significantly – a severe attack could kill it. Trees grown in a greenhouse rarely suffer from peach leaf curl. The problem is more prevalent in damp springs. The problem can be tackled in late winter by spraying with Bordeaux mix, if you wish. Otherwise, pick off the affected leaves and destroy them as soon as possible and ensure the tree has good growing conditions to give it the best chance. A foliar feed with seaweed solution can help give trees a boost. 'Red Haven' is resistant to peach leaf curl.

Split stone If the supply of water to the tree has been erratic then the peach can be holed at the stalk end and the stone inside will be rotted – this is known as split stone. Better irrigation next season is the simple solution.

Silver leaf and bacterial canker can also be a problem (see pages 203–205).

Wasps As with most fruit wasps can be troublesome, boring into the fruit the moment it is ripe. Lessen the allure of the tree by picking ripe fruit regularly and removing any fruit that falls from the tree.

Right *The very dwarfing peach tree 'Bonanza' is a great choice for growing in a container so it can be moved to exploit the warmest spots in the garden and is easily protected. It also has the added benefit that it never needs pruning.*

nectarine

The nectarine is a sport of the peach. Though similar, the trees are more difficult to grow, less productive, and in the main the fruits are smaller than the peach. The fruits are firmer when ripe and lack the soft, suede fuzz of a peache skin. Nectarines need very similar conditions to peaches only better, more accurate watering and ideal temperatures. If your conditions are less than ideal the effort you will have to put in to get what may or may not be a good crop can't be worthwhile. They will grow well in a greenhouse or conservatory where conditions can be controlled, but they do need to be subjected to a cold period to bear fruit.

apricot

Bursting with beta-carotene and deliciously sweet, the velvet-skinned apricot is not as demanding to grow as might be expected. If you are undecided whether to add a peach, nectarine or apricot tree to your garden, then choose the apricot. In many ways apricots are similar to peaches – the trees have a similar appearance, both flower early and so frost and pollination can be problematic, and both need a warm summer to ripen the fruit. In general, however, the apricot's cultivation is much easier. They will fruit on old wood as well as new spurs, so they do not need pruning. They enjoy drier conditions, are not susceptible to peach leaf curl and are less bothered by silver leaf. The problem most likely to be encountered in growing apricots are late frosts.

when will tree bear fruit

3–4 years.

approximate yield

A fan trained tree will yield about 5.5–13.5 kg (12–30 lb).

fruitful years

20–30 years.

cultivars

'Doucouer' This cultivar has the advantage of flowering late. This has two rewards: firstly, the blossom is less likely to be damaged by frost if you are in an area that suffers from late frosts; and secondly, there are likely to be more pollinating insects around. It is very productive and has a delicious flavour.

'Flavorcot' A late flowering apricot with plenty of flavour and a reliable, prodigious crop if the growing conditions are right. This cultivar was bred specifically for the cool climate of the UK.

Left *'Delicot' is closely related to 'Flavorcot' but has a more delicate flavour.*

Above *Choosing apricot trees growing on modern dwarfing rootstocks means trees are easily covered with netting to protect the tender fruit from the birds.*

'Moorpark' For a long time this has been the real stalwart of the apricots. It produces good sized, orangey fruits late in the summer. Exceptionally reliable, though newer cultivars will produce a larger harvest.

'Tomcat' This tree should deliver an exceptional crop of crimson-flushed, delicious fruits.

spacing

Allow 3.5 m (12 ft) between bush trees.

planting

Apricots can begin growing very early in the season so plant them in the autumn. Container grown plants can be planted at any time but will need a great deal of attention to establish successfully in the warmer months. The trees require a stout stake.

apricot

soil and situation

Apricots need a warm summer to ripen successfully. They will crop as free standing areas in a sheltered spot but in cooler areas they will enjoy the microclimate produced by south facing a wall or fence. Apricots do well grown in pots, both inside and out, but they do need a cold resting period to persuade them to fruit. The most important factor for growing good apricots is a well-drained, reasonably light soil. They are winter hardy but in areas with a good deal of rain it pays to add extra drainage when planting and cover the soil around the plant to stop the soil becoming too wet. They will not tolerate an acid soil.

maintenance

In areas with late frosts the blossom will need protection. This is easy with small patio trees – a length of horticultural fleece or any light fabric can be draped over the tree. If the weather is poor when your tree is in bloom, take a moment to notice if there are any pollinating insects about. If there aren't, and you want a good harvest, hand pollination is the only option. It is not difficult, just laborious. Using a small paint brush, dab the centre of as many flowers as you can. If your pollination is a great success you may need to thin the resulting fruitlets by about a quarter.

Feed with an all purpose organic fertilizer in early spring and mulch around the tree. Feed pot grown apricots with an organic tomato food from fruit set to late summer as per the manufacturers instructions.

pruning

Apricots do not require pruning, just chose a tree with a good basic structure. Any dead or diseased wood can be removed if necessary.

when to harvest

A fully ripe apricot will part from the tree without any tugging. Leave the fruits on the tree to ripen to their full-flavoured, un-buyable sweetness. The fruits will ripen at different times, so you will possibly be able to enjoy fresh apricots over a few weeks.

The best way to enjoy apricots is straight from the tree. They will only keep a few days in the cool once picked. Apricots make fine jam and can be frozen if the stone is first removed, although they are really only fit for cooking once defrosted.

problems and solutions

Bacterial canker, birds, and, to a small extent, silver leaf (see page 203), can all affect apricot trees.

Right *The delightful pink blossom of the apricot appears early in the spring and is easily damaged by late frost.*

mulberry

If you want to enjoy your own mulberries you really need space and time. It will probably be about 10 years before your tree will fruit. A mature tree can reach about 10 m (30 ft) tall and occupy valuable garden space, albeit after several years. If you have the room and are willing to wait, the tree is very easy going and when it is mature will produce masses of tasty berries with absolutely no intervention. The trees look good and improve with age.

when will tree bear fruit

5–10 years.

approximate yield

More than you need, eventually.

fruitful years

Hundreds for black mulberry.

cultivars

The black mulberry is usually grown for its fruit, while the white mulberry is typically only grown as silkworm fodder.

planting and spacing

Part of the mulberry tree's appeal is its spreading shape, so it needs a good 10 m (32 ft) chunk of space eventually, hence they really are not a good choice for smaller gardens. They can look majestic set in a large area of lawn. Plant bareroot trees in the dormant season.

soil and situation

The trees will do well in most soils that are reasonably moist and do not suffer from water-logging.

Left *The fruit of the mulberry is not robust and should be handled as little as possible.*

maintenance

Mulch around young trees and feed with a general purpose organic fertilizer in the spring. Water young trees until they get their roots down.

pruning

Buy a well-shaped standard or half standard tree and all you need do is cut out dead or diseased wood.

when to harvest

The fruits are ripe when they are fully black. They can be picked by hand or shaken from the tree onto a sheet placed on the ground. The fruit is incredibly fragile and will not stand up to much handling or washing without becoming mush. Mulberries can be eaten straight from the tree or used to make jam.

problems and solutions

Exceptionally trouble free except that birds will feast on the ripe fruit.

medlar

If you want to eat medlars then you really do have to grow them. Best eaten when they start to decompose, understandably they don't often appear on supermarket shelves. The good news is the spreading medlar tree is quite graceful, with pretty flowers in spring and blazing foliage in the autumn, and it is easy to please. However, they will occupy a good 5 m (16 ft) square of garden to reach their full majesty and will grow to a reasonably lofty 4.5–6 m (15–20 ft) tall. The russet-coloured fruits are left for several weeks after harvest to attain the perfect cider-like, sweet flavour.

when will tree bear fruit

4–6 years old.

approximate yield

Plenty, once establshed.

fruitful years

Very long-lived.

cultivars

'Nottingham' and **'Royal'** are both common and reliable cultivars. 'Royal' produces the larger fruits.
'Large Russian', as its name suggests, has better sized fruits.
'Dutch' has a very spreading habit.

planting and spacing

Allow each tree about 5 m (16 ft) square, though they can be under-planted. I have planted three young trees close together and angled to imitate a multi-stemmed tree as they grow – one crown, three trunks – to give this appealing tree even more character.

soil and situation

It will tolerate almost any soil except that which is water-logged, and will thrive in the sun or partial shade.

maintenance

Mulch annually around the young tree, after a couple of years you can grass up to the tree. After that a handful or two of general-purpose fertilizer should suffice.

pruning

Only prune to remove diseased or damaged wood. The trees have a lovely habit, so it is preferable to plant them in a location where they can develop their natural shape.

when to harvest

Leave the fruit on the tree until mid autumn when it should part from the tree easily. At this point the fruit can be used to make jelly. If you want to eat them they should be kept in a dry, cool place, laid out on trays stalk side up and left for about three weeks to 'blet', or begin to decompose. The flesh will become soft and brownish. An easier way to harvest is to wait for the fruits to drop from the tree and simply collect them up. At this point they will be at least part way through the bletting process, but this route is a little hit and miss.

pests and diseases

Rarely have any problems.

Right *The rather earthy-looking medlar should be picked before the first frosts.*

quince

If you have damp soil that other fruit trees might baulk at, growing quince could be the solution. This hardy tree will even grow on the margins of ponds, but they will do well in regular garden soil and prettier varieties look quite at home amongst ornamental shrubs. Their high pectin content means they make fantastic preserves, but they rarely ripen enough to be eaten raw in cooler climes. The genuine quince should not be confused with chaenomeles which are often referred to as quince.

when will tree bear fruit

3–4 years on the dwarfing quince C rootstock, 4–5 years on quince B.

approximate yield

More than you need once established.

fruitful years

Not long lived.

cultivars

'Vranja Nenodovic' AGM Starts producing pear-shaped fruits early.
'Meech's Prolific' Pear-shaped, well flavoured fruits.

spacing

On quince A, rootstock trees will have a spread of about 3–5 m (10–16 ft). On quince C it will be 3–3.5 m (10–12 ft).

planting

Plant bareroot trees in the dormant period. They should be staked for two years.

soil and situation

Will do best in a sunny, sheltered location with moist, deep, fertile soil. However they will do well on any reasonable garden soil.

Left *Quince do well in damp soil and make delicious preserves due to their high pectin content.*

maintenance

Mulch around the tree with plenty of organic matter to retain moisture, and consider watering even established trees in prolonged dry spells.

pruning

Only remove damaged and diseased wood.

when to harvest

Leave the fruits on the tress as long as possible but pick before the first frosts. The ripe fruit will be yellow and aromatic. Store the aromatic fruits in a cool, dry, dark place and they will gradually become yellow if it has not been warm enough for them to ripen on the tree.

problems and solutions

Quince are relatively trouble free to grow, though they can occasionally suffer from brown rot (see page 203) and powdery mildew.

fig

Succulent, sweet figs are definitely one of the fruits I class as a real indulgence, evocative of Mediterranean sunshine and clear blue skies. In temperate regions, they will fruit well if given the shelter of a south or south-west facing wall, or they will flourish in a container that can be easily protected from frost and moved to benefit from the microclimates around the garden. I grow a wonderful standard fig in a pot which spends the summer on the terrace against a south facing wall, and the winter frost-free in the conservatory. Potted trees can be stashed in a shed or garage so long as they are moved out as soon as the weather warms up. With grey, smooth bark and magnificent, leathery leaves, the fig is a hansome tree with a tropical air. Established trees are wonderfully fruitful and tolerant of neglect. In fact the fig is often called the 'lazy man's fruit'. True perhaps, but the slightly more diligent will reap a more reliable harvest.

when will tree bear fruit

3–4 years.

approximate yield

6.75–9 kg (15–20 lb) bush or fan trained.

fruitful years

Tens of years. The trees can live for hundreds.

cultivars

'Brown Turkey' The most readily available cultivar, probably because it is one of the most reliable in cool climates. The fruits, which are borne in profusion, are brown to purple with red flesh and wonderfully sweet.

'White Marseilles' Will grow outside in cooler areas but will do better if brought inside for the winter. The fruits are large and a warm white-green.

'Violetta' Most resistant to frost, it will survive short periods down to -20°C. Self-fertile. The fruit has sweet, red flesh.

'Brunswick' Delivers a crop of very large fruits on a tree that is one of the hardiest and ideal for colder areas.

spacing

Figs can be grown fairly informally against a wall. Left unchecked, they could spread for as much as 12 or 15 m (40 or 50 ft). If you are willing to put in the work, fan trained figs will eventually occupy a generous 3.5 m (12 ft) of wall space and will reach about 2.5 m (8 ft) tall. Figs are not grafted onto a rootstock to control growth. In open ground or in a pot, figs can be grown as bushes or standards. In open ground a tree might eventually occupy 5–6 square metres (54–65 square foot), but in pots they can be kept much smaller.

Above left *Fig 'White Marseilles'.*

Right *Fig 'Saint John'.*

Above *In the spring, as the fresh leaves unfurl, the embryonic figs that have overwintered on the tree begin to swell to ripen late in the summer. Failure to produce fruit is often caused by frost damage from the previous season.*

fig

planting

If you are planting against a wall dig a hole about 60 x 60 cm (24 x 24 in) wide and 45 cm (17¾ in) deep, and line the sides with old paving slabs or robust slates. To ensure the pit is well-drained, put a good layer of rubble in the base. Fill the pit with a mix of loam-based potting compost and garden soil. Plant the fig away from the base of the wall at a slight angle. Wire strung across the face of the wall, about 30–40 cm (12–16 in) apart, can be used to tie the tree to.

soil and situation

The fig requires a well-drained soil, but it need not be too rich. If the soil is too fertile the tree will be lush and healthy, but will not produce any figs. For the same reason figs that are to be planted directly into the ground should have their root run restricted. Water logged or very damp soils will not suit the sun-loving fig. Give your fig the spot most like the Mediterranean in your plot.

maintenance

Theoretically, the common fig can carry two crops a year. One from the embryonic, pea-sized fruits carried on the youngest growth through the winter that swell to ripen in late summer, and a second which forms in late summer will not ripen in cool climates. The fig tree is robust, hardy to at least -10°C, but the soft young tips and embryonic fruits are the parts most likely to be nipped by frost and this means no figs! It is worth giving the outdoor fig some winter protection in cold areas. A few layers of horticultural fleece should be sufficient, although in extremely cold regions the whole tree can be wrapped. Traditionally, this might be done by constructing a wire framework close to the tree and stuffing it with straw. An easy option is to just protect the vulnerable growth with lengths of foam pipe lagging. Having said all this, I know of trees, probably growing in just the right spot, which brave winter winds unclothed and produce fruit like mad. Figs planted into the ground in a restricting pit will need regular watering in dry conditions and feeding with a tomato liquid feed. Any fig tree in open ground can probably be left to its own devices. Figs in pots require regular watering and feeding weekly with a tomato fertilizer. Protecting the embryonic crop is much easier in potted figs, so long as you can move them to a frost-free garage, shed or cold greenhouse. Just keep the compost very slightly damp. In temperate climates the small figs of the second crop can be removed in the autumn, as they will come to nothing.

pruning

Before you embark upon any pruning it is worthwhile noting that figs can ooze an irritant sap, so wear gloves and long sleeves. Figs can and often are left without pruning when grown outside, and large leggy trees sprawl up walls or buildings. Fig trees left to their own devices will still produce fruit, although the crop may not be as great as if the tree had been regularly pruned, nor will the figs be easy to pick. The tendency is for the fruit to be produced at the ends of the branches while the centre is bare. Eventually, though, such a tree might need renovating by removing some of the oldest branches. This is best done in spring over two or three years. Fan-trained trees should also be pruned in spring, after the last frost.

Established fan-trained trees are pruned by removing any growth heading into or away from the wall. Long, lush shoots can also be removed as short, stubby branches are more fruitful. Pruning can be done at anytime in the dormant period but is best left until very early spring.

If you decide to prune, begin pruning standard trees by removing dead or diseased wood and any suckers. Next take out any crossing or inconveniently-placed branches. Finally, if liked, cut the branches back by a quarter. This concentrates effort on fruiting. Do not radically prune trees whcih have been untouched for years. Tackle in stages, a little each year.

when to harvest

To be at their most mouth-wateringly delicious, figs should be left on the tree until they are completely ripe (one of the reasons figs sold in shops can seldom compare). The fig will be soft, fully coloured and the eye at the base will open slightly. If the figs are a little mealy, they are not ripe.

problems and solutions

Birds and wasps are partial to figs, particularly if the fruits become overripe, so pick regularly, clear fallen fruit and net the trees if birds are a problem.
Leaf loss Figs react to drought in the summer by dropping all their leaves. It looks final but a given a good supply of water they should come back into growth. This is more common in container-grown figs. I have experienced a large container-grown tree shedding virtually all but its youngest leaves, only to quickly return to health when its water supply was adjusted.
Red spider mite and cankers See page 205.

nuts

When planning a productive garden, nut trees are seldom high on the list of plants to include. However, if you are looking for minimum maintenance, are willing to wait a few years for your first harvest and have the space, creating a nuttery or just adding a few attractive nut trees to the garden is a sensible option. Most nut trees are majestic and handsome and can hold their own against many ornamental varieties. They are relatively trouble-free and, once established, supply an abundance of protein-packed nuts. Just select the right trees for your situation and wait.

Left *Expect to start harvesting cob and filbert nuts about three or four years after planting, if you start with one year old whips.*

Right *A mature sweet chestnut tree.*

filbert and cobnuts

These trees are real survivors, tolerant of neglect, and are deliverers of a bountiful harvest for little effort. Ideal for those who want an easy life. However, the biggest problem is protecting the nuts from squirrels, who will effortlessly strip the trees. I once heard the only way to ensure a good crop for the gardener to enjoy was to grow more trees than the local squirrel population can eat. A little impractical for most of us. The other option is to grow the trazel, a hybrid of the Turkish hazel and the common European hazel (see below). They can be grown on a trunk with a squirrel-proof baffle, which will work so long as the squirrels can't jump from nearby trees.

If you are short of space, the bushy cob and filbert can be kept to just 1.8–2.5 m (6–8 ft) tall and still deliver a good crop – if you get to them before the squirrels, that is. There are even some beautifully decorative cultivars which really do look quite at home amongst ornamental shrubs, such as the red filbert with its long purple red catkins, purple foliage and red shelled nuts. These hardy nuts will grow on the poorest of soils and crop generously despite neglect.

cultivars

'Kentish Cob', also known as **'Lambert's Filbert'**, is widely available. It produces a good crop of lovely, long, large nuts.

'Red Filbert' More decorative than many ornamental shrubs, the red filbert injects a vibrant burst of colour into the garden with its large red leaves, ruddy nuts and frilly husks. Grown as a multi-stemmed shrub.

'Webb's Prize Cobnut' Hailed as tough enough to make a good, productive windbreak, this vigorous variety produces nuts similar to the 'Kentish Cob'.

'Hall's Giant Cobnut' Another toughy that is prolific, too. Requires cross pollination.

Trazels A hybrid of the European cob and the Turkish cob. These are non-suckering and grow into fair sized trees. They are more easily grown on a trunk and so can be protected from squirrels with baffle. Named trazels include Chinoka and Laroka.

Grow two or more varieties to ensure successful pollination, although if there are some wild cobs in the area they will do the job nicely.

planting and spacing

Bareroot plants can be planted in the dormant season. Container-grown plants can be planted at any time. Staking is not needed except on very exposed sites. The space between plants will depend to some degree on how you intend to grow them. Bushes pruned to keep them small can be just 2.5 m (8 ft) apart, while larger bushes will need 4.5 m (15 ft) space.

soil and situation

Completely unfussy so long as the soil is not water logged. Slightly acid and slightly alkaline soils are fine. In fact, very rich soil may cause a problem, as the tree will be a picture of health but unproductive. A sunny spot is best – they will grow reasonably well in a shadier location but will probably be less productive.

maintenance

These plants require little care. A few handfuls of general purpose fertilizer early in spring and a good layer of mulch in the first couple of years will help them to establish.

pruning

This is where things can seem a little trickier, but they need not be. Hazels are traditionally 'brutted' in the late summer. This encourages fruit buds to form and all it involves is partially snapping strong shoots about 30 cm (12 in) from their tip so they hang down. If you don't do this, your tree should still produce nuts, but just not in such profusion. The easiest way to

Right *These nuts are a way off being ready for picking. The husks are papery and yellow when the nuts are ripe.*

Above *An orchard of hazel trees with a traditional wooden orchard ladder.*

filbert and cobnuts

grow hazels is as a bush, relatively untouched, but they can be grown as a more open goblet shape on a short trunk. Pruning is done in the winter. Leaders can be cut back by half and remaining laterals to four buds.

Remember, even if you do nothing, your hazel will produce nuts. It will re-grow quickly even if pruned badly or just plain hacked back because it is in the way.

when to harvest

You know hazels are ripe when they fall off. Harvesting then becomes a simple matter of gathering them up. If the bushes are in an area of rough grass, cut the grass back before the nuts ripen to make them easier to collect. To keep well the nuts need to be dried. Remove the husks and spread the nuts on a tray somewhere warm. The husks should come away easily from ripe nuts, although some varieties are more challenging than others. Once dry they can be stored in hessian bags or net sacks in a cool dry place.

problems and solutions

Squirrels are the biggest problem. The only way to foil them is to secure baffles, something shiny and slippery that can't be scaled by squirrels, wrapped around hazels grown on a decent trunk. Trazels are well suited to this form. Ensure the squirrels cannot jump into the hazel from neighbouring trees.

Nut weevils A small hole in the shell is the tell-tale sign that the maggot of the nut weevil has hatched effectively inside the nut, eaten its fill and bored its way out. These weevils are unlikely to be a major problem in the garden.

walnut

The walnut is a magnificent tree. The largest will reach a towering 30 m (100 ft) or more, while most will achieve 10 m (32 ft) in their first 20 years. Grafted trees are the wise choice. They will provide a crop quickly, the nuts will be good quality and their growth pattern and size can be more accurately predicted. These splendid trees are very straightforward to grow; the hardest thing about enjoying home-grown walnuts is processing the nuts. The nuts grow within a green fleshy hull, the sap within the hull stains hands, gloves, clothes, and even wood, black (it can be used as a natural hair dye). Before the nuts can be stored this hull has to be removed. Even though it splits open as the nuts ripen, it is a bit fiddly and messy. There are two species of walnut: the Persian or English walnut, grown for its edible nuts, and the heartier black walnut from North America, which produces nuts which are not so good to eat,

so it is worth checking what you are buying.

when will tree bear fruit

Grafted trees 3–4 years, non-grafted 12 years.

approximate yield

65 kg (145 lb).

fruitful years

100 upwards.

cultivars

'Broadview' A strong compact tree which is known for its easy-going nature and good crop. Resistant to walnut tree blight.
'Rita' Is especially useful where space is limited, though it still reaches a lofty 8 m (26 ft) at maturity.
'Plovdivski' A prolific Bulgarian variety which produces large fruit on a tough tree. Blight-resistant.
'Metcalfe' Produces a rather thin-shelled, early ripening nut.

spacing

In placing a walnut tree you not only have to think about how much space it will occupy, but how it will influence the plants around it. Its roots produce a chemical (juglone) which inhibits the growth of many other plants. This effectively means that nothing can be cultivated successfully in the area influenced by the tree's roots, which you can judge as about the same as the extent of the tree's canopy. As the tree grows, this no-grow area will grow with it. Some plants will survive, but they will probably be stunted. Some plants are reportedly immune, but I have seen plants on both the survivors and the non-survivors lists of different sources. Shallow-rooted plants may well be less affected. Planting a good 12–18 m (42–59 ft) from other plants might be reasonable. However, I have an ancient walnut tree, and within its influence there is a burgeoning native hedgerow, a thriving neatly clipped beech hedge and various shrubs.

planting

The trees are best planted bareroot in the dormant season with the soil at the same level they were grown in the nursery. Container plants can be added to the garden at anytime, but will need plenty of care and water if planted in the summer until they establish. It is even more important than usual that the container-grown walnut has not been in its pot for too long and become pot bound, as they produce a long tap root. They will only need a short stake for the first couple of years.

soil and situation

These trees thrive in heavy moist soil, but will do well in most soil types. I have one growing convincingly on a very free-draining soil. The trees are best planted where they can enjoy the sun, as the nuts will not ripen if the site is too shaded. The trees are fully hardy but young growing tips are susceptible to damage from late frosts so avoid planting trees in frost pockets.

walnut

maintenance

Mature trees are unlikely to need much attention, but it is important that young trees are not allowed to dry out, especially in the early spring. A good layer of organic matter will help to retain moisture for the first couple of years.

pruning

Prune in late autumn. Buy a nicely-shaped tree and leave it to grow. Ideally walnut trees should be left without pruning to attain a natural shape. However, dead or badly placed branches can be removed in late autumn.

when to harvest

Young nuts can be picked for pickling before the shell inside the husk hardens. This will be in early to midsummer. If squirrels are a problem in your garden this may be the only way you can enjoy your walnuts, taking them before the squirrels find them irresistible.

Picking up fallen walnuts from the ground is the easiest method of harvest. To avoid too much bending use a nut picker, a sphere made of parallel wires on a long handle which, when pushed along the ground, gives to allow the nuts to pop into the sphere. Some advocate knocking the nuts from the tree with a stick, but this becomes impossible with large trees.

One of the main problems with enjoying home-grown walnuts is getting at them. The nuts grow in a green fleshy husk around the hard shell, and these husks become black with age. Although they split, the husk is not always easily removed from the nutshell and it leaves a black stain on hands, clothes and under nails that can take days to scrub away, so always wear gloves to collect walnuts. The husk must be removed before the nuts can be stored, and this is a laborious task. Some people pick them off, some hammer the nuts through holes in a board just the right size to allow the nut through and leave the husk behind. All very time consuming. Once clean the walnuts need to be dried, preferably in the sun, and can then be stored in airy boxes in a cool dry place.

Left and above *The ripe walnut is held within a tough husk which has to be removed before the nuts can be stored.*

pests and diseases

These are fairly trouble-free trees.

Walnut leaf blight Black spots appear on leaves, stems and fruits. There is nothing that can be done to eradicate the effects of this bacterium. Its spread can be limited by removing and destroying infected leaves.

Walnut blotch This causes dead brown patches on the leaves which fall earlier than would be expected. It is caused by a fungal disease which spends the winter in fallen leaves. Nothing can be done beyond clearing the fallen leaves and destroying them.

sweet chestnut

The plump, sweet, smooth and succulent flesh of the sweet chestnut is irresistible raw and even more appealing roasted. The only snag is that trees can reach a towering 30 m (100 ft) – too big for most gardens. To get good-sized nuts the summer needs to be a good one, with plenty of heat and sunshine.

The tree is undoubtedly appealing, with large rigid leaves, a deeply grooved bark and the fresh green, long spiked husks of the nuts. When mature the trees are pretty much the perfect tree, commanding and statuesque, but sadly more suited to parkland than the average garden. Trees grow to 10 m (32 ft) in 20 years.

approximate yield

At least 10 kg (22 lb) once the tree reaches 10 years old.

fruitful years

The trees can produce nuts for hundreds of years.

cultivars

Often the sweet chestnut is only available as the species, in other words you will just be buying a 'sweet chestnut' tree, rather than a named cultivar.
'Regal' Smaller than the traditional sweet chestnut, this cultivar can be accommodated in a largish garden. It is extremely compact and at 10 years will only reach 4.5 m (15 ft).

soil and situation

Reputed to prefer lighter loamy soils or light sandy soils, although I have them growing well in clay. They will tolerate some acidity and will grow on alkaline soils.

pruning

No pruning is required (unless branches become damaged) to preserve the tree's natural shape.

problems and solutions

Mostly trouble-free, although large birds and squirrels will take the nuts. In America chestnut blight has almost put an end to the American Sweet Chestnut, and resistant hybrids should be grown there.

Above left *Chestnuts are the only nuts to contain vitamin C.*

Right *The spiky casings of the unripe chestnut are tightly closed, splitting as the nut ripens.*

other fruits

There are a number of fruits that do not fit neatly into any of the previous groups. They also have little in common with each other in their cultivation, and in reality one (rhubarb) is actually not even a fruit. However, for convenience, this disparate group are assembled here. They are no less worthy of garden space, nor are they more testing or less rewarding to grow.

Left *In the autumn 'Kempsey Black' ignites in a blaze of autumn colours as green gives way to vivid, show-stopping orange and crimson.*

Right *A kiwi vine provides shelter and protection for this bird box.*

grape

Grapes can be amongst the simplest fruit to grow or the most exacting, depending on how you choose to grow them. There are entire volumes devoted to how to grow grapes, perhaps because of their central role in wine making, but growing grapes in the average garden need not be difficult. The first important step to growing grapes with ease is choosing the right vine for your location. Some vines will only thrive under glass in temperate climates whilst others will be fruitful outside in colder areas. Choosing how to train your vine will determine how much time you will need to invest. If you are hoping for a vine to provide a Mediterranean-style shade over a pergola and a few grapes, then simply plant and leave it untamed to scramble over the structure. Similarly, a carefully chosen vine left to smother a warm trellis or fence will provide fruit, decorative foliage and dramatic autumn colour. In the conservatory the grape vine can be left to explore walls and ceilings, providing some natural shade for other plants.

The alternative is to choose one of the many methods of training a vine – the cordon, multiple cordon, guyot, double guyot, standard or espalier, to mention but a few – and gen up on the corresponding pruning method. None are simple and probably fall within the domain of the enthusiast. For those in pursuit of easy fruit I whole heartedly recommend the far less formal approach described here.

when will plant bear fruit

3 years old.

approximate yield

6.75 kg (15 lb).

fruitful years

Around 40 years.

cultivars

Indoor

'Black Hamburg' A real favourite, probably because it produces great grapes and is truly easygoing. The sweet berries are dark purple with a dusty, white bloom and will ripen even if the temperature is not high.
'Golden Chasselas' A good choice for container growing, it produces small, white grapes in profusion. Good for eating and wine making.
'Lakemont' Good sized bunches of grapes, resistant to mildew.

Outdoor

'Leon Millot' Very hardy outdoor variety. Produces a good crop of black grapes mid season on a very vigorous vine that is resistant to mildew.
'Brandt' If your motivation is as much to disguise an ugly structure or fence in foliage as it is to have a few grapes for the table, then choose this vine. Although the grapes are tiny and held in smallish bunches, the plant will grow at a stunning pace so long as it is in a sunny spot. It puts on a truly sizzling display of autumn colour. It even has some mildew resistance.
'Perlette' Another vigorous vine for a warm wall producing small, yellowish seedless grapes.

soil and situation

Vines grown outside need plenty of sun and a warm sheltered location. South, south-east and south-west facing walls or fences are ideal, as are pergolas located on the sunny side of the house or arches and obelisks that are bathed in sun and away from cold winds. The ideal soil is gritty and well-drained with plenty of organic matter.

spacing

One vine, given time, will engulf most structures, and you could speed matters along by planting vines about 2 m (6½ ft) apart.

Right *Grown outside, grapes need plenty of sun and warmth to ripen. A south-facing wall is the perfect spot.*

grape

planting

Vines are often offered container-grown and can be added to the garden at any time of year, although early autumn or early spring are best. Mulch around the vine lavishly with some good garden compost after planting and tie the main stems into the structure.

maintenance

Water regularly until vines are well established. Vines under glass will need watering more or less every day during the growing season. They will also need a period of cold in the winter to fruit well. Outside, mulch with well-rotted organic matter and feed each spring with all purpose organic fertilizer at the rate recommended by the manufacturer.

There is a fiddly but simple bit of work you might like to try to ensure your grapes are of a good size. It is not essential, fairly laborious but almost therapeutic. When the grapes are pea-sized, use a small, sharp pair of scissors reduce the number of grapes in the bunch by about 50 per cent, taking grapes spread evenly over the bunch – tedious yet easy, but not essential. As a result the berries will be fewer, larger and juicier.

pruning

The relaxed, easy method of growing grapes expounded here is obviously not as efficient as the skilfully pruned vine, though most years you get a stunning plant and eventually a worthwhile crop. Although the exacting pruning methods can be forgotten, there will be a little cutting back to do eventually, if anything just to keep the vine within the confines of its allotted space. Once it is established, and before it gets out of hand, just cut back any congested or stray growth. No skill required. The only important point to remember is not to hack at it in the summer as the vine will bleed and become weakened.

when to harvest

Leave the grapes on the vine to ripen fully. The main problem in achieving this will be the birds, which peck at the grapes, and wasps, which make use of the damage done by the birds. Wait until the grapes are full, plump and evenly coloured. Having a quick taste is the most reliable check of how ripe dessert grapes might be.

Above *This beautifully trained vine will have taken years of careful pruning to develop and maintain this shape.*

Left *A vigorous grape vine has been left to romp the length of this pergola with spectacular effect.*

problems and solutions

Powdery mildew This is usually spotted at the end of the growing season as a white powder of the youngest growth. At this point it is nothing to worry about as the leaves will soon drop, just clear away the affected foliage. It is usually caused by a lack of water, so up the irrigation in the following year.

kiwi

Also known as the Chinese gooseberry, the kiwi is a climbing vine which produces greenish-brown, fuzzy fruits that have a fresh flavour and are packed with vitamin C. The vine has robust leaves. Fine, radiant red hair covers the stems and its flowers are pretty, white and fragrant. Left unchecked, it can grow to about 10 m (32 ft) tall supporting itself by spiralling around anything that might aid its upward progress. The kiwi thrives in a warm, sunny spot, climbing against a wall, stout trellis or over a pergola. In a favourable location the kiwi vine will grow very quickly into a heavy, tangled mass if left without pruning and training. They are one of the few fruiting plants that really will not do well in a container because of their natural vigour; they may survive for a year or two but are unlikely to be as productive.

Originally kiwi plants were not self-fertile. There were male and female plants, and one male plant would need to be grown for every six or so females. The pollination process can be a bit hit and miss if the male plant fails to do well. Now there are self-fertile varieties, this is a much easier option. You only need to grow one plant and the results should be excellent, although these may still do better if they have other cultivars for cross-pollination.

when will plant bear fruit

4–5 years (garden centre plants are usually 2–3 years old).

approximate yield

A mature vine in the right spot could yield up to 45 kg (100 lb).

fruitful years

Peak at 6–8 years.

cultivars

'Solo' Self-fertile cultivar, a vigorous grower which produces a good number of fruits, though they are not large.
'Jenny' Popular self-fertile variety.
'Hayward' Widely available female cultivar but requires the presence of a male to produce fruits. One male plant to five female.
'Tomuri' A male plant known to be a good pollinator.

soil and situation

Though the vines probably do best against a sunny wall, they will tolerate some shade. They are reasonably unfussy about soil, but do need good drainage or they can suffer from root rot.

maintenance

In addition to a layer of organic matter around the plant in autumn or spring, good fruit production can be ensured by using a liquid feed (seaweed would be ideal) from flowering until the fruits are harvested. Once established, kiwis do not need a great deal of water except in periods of drought.

pruning

Prune sometime after the fruit is picked and before spring. Fruits are borne on the side shoots on canes which are one year old or more, but the older the cane the less productive it becomes. Once it is four years old a cane has probably given its best and can be dispensed with. So the strategy is to cut out all canes that are four years old to ground level. Sounds simple, but as you approach the thicket that your kiwi vine may well become it may not be so. Don't panic – look at the plant, some canes will look much older than others, and remove the canes that appear oldest.

when to harvest

The fruits are ripe when the dull green skin becomes slightly brown and darker and gives a little when gently squeezed. This is usually in late summer or early autumn.

problems and solutions

None of the common pests and diseases trouble the kiwi, making it a joy to grow. The only thing that can disturb its robust constitution is prolonged damp at the roots.

Above *Immature kiwi 'Jenny'.*

Right *Kiwi 'Hayward'.*

melon

If I invest time and effort in growing something to eat, I expect it to taste better than shop-bought. Not only is home-grown melon tastier, it is truly spectacular. Too often melons are just a bit disappointing, watery with little taste, like eating slightly sweet mush. Pick the right cultivar and the honey scent of melon will fill the air as it ripens and the melting flesh will be filled with astounding, sweet flavours. Melons do require a little more attention than other fruit. It is a tropical climbing plant and so needs good temperatures and humidity, and you can really only allow four fruits to ripen on each plant, perhaps six if conditions are perfect, so you will not bag a massive harvest, but it is worth it. There are cultivars adapted to colder climes but if temperatures are not consistently warm in your area, they are better grown in a greenhouse or conservatory. Their general requirements are much like cucumbers.

when will plant bear fruit

First year (annual plant).

approximate yield

4 fruits.

fruitful years

Grown as an annual.

cultivars

'Sweetheart' Is a charantais-type melon that is hardier than most fast-growing early melons, with wonderfully sweet and fragrant orange flesh. Suited to growing outside and under glass.
'Snow leopard' Produces small pale fruits. It is a honeydew melon with a good flavour and will grow in less than perfect weather.
'Superlative' A musk melon, only suited to a heated greenhouse, it has a green skin and red succulent flesh

Melon plants are now available grafted onto incredibly vigorous rootstocks, usually of those of an ornamental gourd, which make them very productive and easy to

Above *Fashioned from the netting bag some avocados were packaged in this homespun hammock supports the melon as it swells and ripens.*

Left *'Sweetheart' is an amazing tasty and reliable performer.*

manage. However, if the melon plant is weak or damaged, the rootstock will take over, as has happened to me once, and will swamp an area at great speed.

soil and situation

Melons require plenty of warmth. In areas that enjoy an almost Mediterranean climate, they will flourish if left to scramble over the soil in open ground. In slightly less favourable conditions they may do well outside if they are covered with a cloche or fleece at night, or grown in a cold frame. In cooler areas, however, melons will only reward you with good fruit if grown against a warm, sunny wall or in pot on a sheltered terrace or under glass. Melons can be grown from seed but buying small plants is a real timesaver and avoids the many pitfalls of coaxing a seed into life.

Left *A melon should not be picked until it is completely ripe – it will come away from the plant when gently lifted.*

Right *Melons perform well if grown up an obelisk in a conservatory. The foliage is bold and dramatic in contrast to the pretty, sunshine-yellow flowers it produces.*

melon

Melons like plenty of organic matter and good moist soil. For ease they can be planted in a growbag set on its end, so long as they are kept well watered and given a regular liquid feed, all purpose initially and tomato food once the fruits have set and begin to swell.

planting and spacing

Small plants to be trained up a trellis or strings can be planted about 60 cm (24 in) apart, or a single plant will do well in a 30–50 cm (12–18 in) pot. If they are to be left to roam free outside, allow each plant about one square metre/yard. If you are planting small plants outside harden them off first, that is getting them accustomed to outside temperatures for a few days by putting them out in the day and bringing them in at night. Melons are planted out in early summer after all risk of frosts has passed.

maintenance

Melon plants are hungry and need plenty of water. However, only water the plants sparingly until they are established as the soft young stems are prone to rot if they are kept too damp. Feed with organic liquid tomato food once a week once the fruits are formed.

The melon plant should make a prodigious amount of growth. It has large leaves and perky, little yellow flowers. Once a melon has formed on a side shoot, nip out the growing tip leaving just two leaves beyond the melon. This allows the plant to put all its efforts into making luscious fruit rather than unnecessary leaves. If a plant produces more than four or five melons, remove any others that form.

As the fruits swell, it is as well to support them in some kind of netting hammock. This can be made from anything that will allow air to circulate, stretch a little as the fruit grows and support the weight of the melon. For plants growing on the soil, lift fruits onto a tile or something similar to keep them off the soil.

when to harvest

When the melon is ripe it will separate from the plant when lifted gently. This is one of the reasons why it is important to support the fruit with nets. Melons are at their best if left on the plant until fragrantly ripe, but they may drop from the plant unexpectedly.

problems and solutions

Neck rot is the most likely problem, where the plant simply rots away where it reaches the soil. This is the result of too much water or cold temperatures.

passion fruit

Grown in many gardens for its stunning flowers with little thought for its fruit, the passion fruit is remarkably easy to grow given the right spot. In fact they are incredibly rampant, potentially climbing 10 m (32 ft), making them a good choice for covering sunny walls and trellis work. Plant breeders have developed many ornamental vines, but 'Passiflora edulis' is the best for producing fruit. There are a plethora of cultivars and some are hardier than others. The less hardy are best grown in pots so they can be brought under cover in the winter and relocated to the warmest part of the garden for the summer. As a rule, all passion fruit need a winter temperature in excess of 10°C and fruit set may be poor in areas where the temperature falls below 16°C. Purple-fruited cultivars will flourish at slightly lower temperatures than those with yellow fruits. In colder areas they can be grown under glass all year round, although this does mean more maintenance with regular watering and feeding to keep the vine at its best. The wrinkled fruit yield a seedy pulp which is sweet and fragrant, and makes an instant fruit sauce for ice cream and pavlova.

Above *It seems unlikely that such magnificently intricate flowers can be borne in such abundance.*

Left *The wrinkled skin of the passion fruit hides a profusion of seeds covered in sweet pulp.*

when will plant bear fruit

One or two years after planting, depending on the climate.

approximate yield

Anything up to a hundred fruits per vine.

fruitful years

8 to 15 years.

cultivars

'Crackerjack' Purple-fruited variety that produces plenty of flowers, making it a pleasure to grow.

spacing

If you want to grow more than one vine space the plants at least 3 m (10 ft) apart.

planting

The vine is a tendril climber and will successfully scramble its way to great heights, but it needs something to climb – walls and fences need to be furnished with wires or trellis. Ensure any support is up to the task. Plant in early summer when temperatures are beginning to rise. Plants in containers can be provided with a large obelisk or cane wigwam. Encourage the plant to take the long route to the top by spiralling growth around the structure.

passion fruit

soil and situation

This subtropical vine really does need a frost-free, warm wall. If the worst happens and the plant gets caught by the frost, clear the dead material away and the vine will probably regrow from the root. Apart from its temperature requirements the plant really isn't fussy. Any reasonable, well-drained soil will do.

maintenance

Water and feed plants in containers regularly using an organic tomato fertilizer. Plants in the ground should be given a good layer of mulch in the early spring and watered in dry periods, particularly if they are planted in the dry area at the base of a wall.

pruning

No pruning required beyond keeping the plant under control. Stray new growth can be cut back in late winter. Left unchecked for some time, the passion fruit can get out of hand. In this situation they can be cut back hard.

when to harvest

Passion fruit look wrinkled and fully coloured (either purple or yellow) when ripe. The easiest way to harvest is to wait for the fruit to fall from the plant. The skin protects the fruit from damage and you know the fruit is perfectly ripe. Where vines have scaled tall buildings, this may be the only option. Fruits should be collected daily and can be stored, sealed in a plastic bag, in a cool place for two to three weeks. The pulp can be scraped from the skins and frozen.

problems and solutions

Plants kept inside may be affected by whitefly or red spider mite. If the plants are mobile, placing them outside for a few days may solve the problem.

rhubarb

First of all I have to acknowledge that the part of the rhubarb plant that is eaten is not a fruit, it is a stem, but from a culinary perspective it is treated as a fruit. It is amazingly easy to grow and tastes delicious. Rhubarb is winter-hardy, drought tolerant, will endure some shade and needs the minimum of attention. It is a cinch to grow and a must-have in the fruit garden, so long as you enjoy its tart flavour. If you are not planning on a dedicated fruit garden, a crown of rhubarb can be slotted into an ornamental bed or it will obligingly grow well in a large container. The only minor trial for a real rhubarb lover is that the stems produced in the first year must be left alone so young plants can build up a good root system and become well established.

Above *An old chimney pot stuffed with a little straw makes an excellent rhubarb forcer.*

when will plant bear fruit

Stems can be harvested in the second year.

approximate yield

This depends on whether you pull slender, short storks or leave them to develop. One or two crowns should be enough for most.

fruitful years

8 to 15 years.

cultivars

'Champagne' Crops over a long season and is suited to forcing.
'Stockbridge Arrow' Reliable cultivar producing good quality, red sticks.
'The Sutton' Late cultivar producing a wealth of very red sticks.
'Timperly Early' A great favourite and one of the earliest to crop. Brilliantly vigorous, throwing up a profusion of slender, pinkish stems. It is excellent for forcing. An early cultivar.
'Victoria' Has a particularly high yield of very large, good-quality stalks. A late cultivar.

spacing

Allow plants about 1 square metre/yard per plant.

planting

Rhubarb is often planted as divisions split from a dormant crown – an unpromising lumpy clump of fibrous material – during the winter. Set these in the ground so that the buds are just level with the surface of the soil. Despite appearances, within a month or so the planted crowns will be throwing up stout red stalks topped with enormous leaves. They should establish quickly but don't be tempted to harvest in year one. Leave the plant to establish, and even in the second year pick only lightly.

soil and situation

Rhubarb is really not fussy about its soil, so long as it gets a good dose of organic material dug in when it is planted and as mulch (preferably well rotted manure) during its dormant period. If you apply mulch annually to all your beds, this will do the trick. If you can provide it with deep, rich, well-drained soil, you will get the best rhubarb possible. If your soil drains

Left *This unpromising clump of severed roots is a crown of rhubarb. It arrived with four others in a small box sealed in a plastic bag. Unlikely as it seems, poked into the soil roots down and the top of the crown level with the surface of the soil, it will soon be throwing up shiny red stems.*

Right *With just a good layer of garden compost or well-rotted manure applied once a year, steadfast rhubarb delivers wonderfully tart stalks for dessert.*

rhubarb

badly, the crowns should be planted on a good-sized ridge or in a raised bed.

maintenance

Beyond applying mulch and tidying up the debris in the autumn, there is really not much to do bar harvesting, except if you want a very early crop. This requires nothing more arduous than putting an up-turned bucket, chimney pot, or, if you are lucky enough to own one, a terracotta rhubarb forcing jar, over a crown during the winter. Stuff the jar or bucket with straw and very early in the spring you will be harvesting the pale, succulent stems that forcing produces. Force plants in rotation, giving each plant a couple of years off.

If your plants produce flower stems (these will look very different to the normal stems), remove them. After four or five years you can divide your original crown. Just chop it with a spade, ensuring each chunk has at least one bud, and re-plant sections of the crown.

pruning

Rhubarb requires no pruning.

when to harvest

As soon as stems are a good size in early spring they can be harvested, continuing into midsummer. Hold the stick low down and twist it away from the plant. Do not be tempted to over-pick, always leave a few sticks and allow the plants to regenerate during the late summer.

Rhubarb freezes well. Chop the sticks into short chunks, tray freeze them then seal them in plastic bags.

problems and solutions

Rhubarb is a really trouble free. Very occasionally it can become infected with a virus, causing the stems to become thin and the plant will look very unhealthy. There is nothing that can be done except to dig up the plant and destroy it. Do not replant rhubarb in the same spot.

almost wild

There is plenty of fruit to be had from the hedgerows and countryside if you feel like foraging. It is worth noting that the trees that fruit without any cultivation will do the same in your garden. While they might not have the all the allure of cultivated soft fruits, they make great preserves and beverages and are good for attracting wildlife.

sloes

The humble sloe looks much like a miniature damson or puffed up blueberry, but anyone who has bitten one will recall their unpleasant, mouth-drying bitterness. A favourite childhood game was to introduce the unsuspecting and uninitiated to the taste of this 'lovely' berry. The sloe is the fruit of the blackthorn tree, commonly found in hedgerows – a tough, scrubby, spiny tree, it cannot be called attractive. However, the trees are real survivors, need no care, will grow in the poorest of soils, are excellent for wildlife and a must for lovers of sloe gin. They are used to make a whole range of pickles and preserves. Blackthorn makes a practical hedge and a stout windbreak. Left to their own devices trees could grow to about 10 m (32 ft) tall.

rowan

The rowan, or mountain ash, is a statuesque tree with attractive flowers, pretty foliage and scorching autumn colours. It produces clusters of fiery scarlet berries each autumn which are often just left to feed the birds, despite the fact they can be used to make tasty preserves and jellies. The trees are very easy to please, growing well anywhere except in areas with very limy soil. When mature the rowan can reach 15 m (50 ft). It requires no pruning and is best left to assume its natural shape.

elder

The elder is a very decorative tree. In the spring it is covered with sprays of white, foamy blossom and these become bunches of glossy, black berries in early autumn. The berries and flowers have culinary uses, making wine, cordial and even champagne. It is unfussy about soil type and while it will grow large if allowed, it can easily be restricted in height.

Left *The striking and decorative berries of the rowan tree.*

how to grow

There are just a few very basic techniques and processes you need to master to grow your own fruit – planting, applying mulch, weeding (and how to avoid it), watering, pruning (depending on your choices), making compost and, if the worst happens, how to deal with pests and diseases.

planting

Once the planning is done, the plants chosen and the ground prepared, at last it is time to get on with the business of gardening and get the plants in the ground. Everything that has gone before is essential. Planning with brightly illustrated catalogues spread before you is exciting, preparing the area or building beds can be hard work but satisfying, but actually setting out the plants and planting them has to be the most rewarding. It is also where all the previous hard work can go wrong. Planting is child's play, but you do need to take a little care. Provide stakes if needed, spread roots carefully and wait until ground conditions are right. Never try to plant into frozen or water-logged ground.

bareroot or container grown plants?

Fruit trees and shrubs can be bought in two ways – grown in pots or bareroot. Plants grown in pots are available all year round while bareroot plants can only be planted in the winter or dormant season. Starting with each type of plant has its benefits; if you are planning a reasonably sized fruit garden there is a natural, practical and reasonably leisurely chain of events that culminates in planting most trees and shrubs bareroot in the winter. The garden can be built or marked out in the good weather of the summer; the soil can be improved into the autumn ready for planting in the late autumn or early winter. If you are planting in bulk then the cost saving advantages of starting with bareroot plants will be appealing too. If you are adding a few fruit trees or bushes to an established garden then container grown plants may fit the bill.

bareroot trees and bushes

Arguably the best and most inexpensive way to plant fruit trees and bushes is as bareroot plants in the winter. Buying bareroot normally offers a greater choice of varieties, and a bareroot tree will actually have a better root system than a tree or bush that has had its roots confined by a container. Bareroot means the plants are grown in the ground in a nursery and lifted in the winter when the plants are dormant, and either dispatched immediately or kept in a cold store until required. When the plants arrive they look like a fairly unpromising bunch of dead sticks with some roots at the end. But planted with care they should establish quickly and grow well in the spring.

Though the bareroot plants appear completely inert, protect the roots from being damaged by cold and drying winds. If the bareroot plants arrive before you are ready to plant them, or when the ground is frozen or too wet to plant them out, they can be 'heeled in'. This means digging a trench deep enough to cover the roots, placing the plants into the trench leaning against its side, and backfilling the trench. If you have nowhere suitable to heel in plants protect the roots with a layer of compost (straw, perhaps) in a large pot or perforated sack and stash the plants in a cool but frost-free place.

Despite the seeming impossibility of lifeless bareroot plants ever sprouting leaves, let alone luscious fruits, I have very seldom had a bareroot fruit plant fail. Taking on plants grown in neat pots, with a well established, compost clad root system, may seem rather less unnerving, but in fact planted in the late autumn bareroot plants will undoubtedly make better plants.

Right *Bought mail order, these well established, container grown plants will grow quickly once planted.*

planting a bareroot fruit bush

1 Plant bareroot plants as soon as possible after they arrive or heel them in. Soak bareroot raspberry canes in a bucket of water for an hour or so before planting.

2 Use sharp clean secateurs to trim any long roots to about 20 cm (8 in) in length to encourage new roots to grow and the canes to establish quickly.

3 In prepared soil dig a slot about 5–7.5 cm (2–3 in) deep. Raspberry canes should not be planted too deeply – use the soil mark on the canes as a guide. Planting at the correct depth encourages the formation of new canes.

4 Space the canes along the trench, 30–45 cm (12–17¾ in) apart. Back-fill the trench with soil and firm it around the canes, leaving them standing upright. If needed, trim the canes to about 30 cm (12 in) tall. Water in the canes. Finally the bed can be finished with a mulch of garden compost, or well rotted manure. If you are planting more than one row, allow 1.5–2 m (5–6½ ft) between rows.

planting bareroot fruit trees

1 Water the tree well before planting. Dig a hole just a little larger in circumference than the pot the tree is growing in, and the same depth. It is important not to plant the tree too deeply and to ensure the graft is well above soil level, or the top part of the tree may begin to grow its own roots rather than being supplied and controlled by the roots it has been grafted onto.

2 Mix a little organic slow release fertilizer into the soil from the hole. Remove the tree from its pot, place it in the hole and back-fill the hole. If the tree appears pot-bound gently free some of the roots around the edge of the root ball.

3 Firm the soil around the root ball to ensure there are no airpockets (you can tread quite heavily on the soil you have replaced working around the tree). If necessary add more soil and repeat.

4 Finally, drive a stake into the ground just beyond the root ball of the tree at a 45° angle, so it is just a few centimetres away from the trunk of the tree. Then attach the tree to the stake. There are many types of tree tie available, all should provide a cushion between the tree and stake to prevent damage to the bark of the tree. Buckle and strap ties are common but here a simple, flexible rubber covered tie in a figure of eight is used.

container grown plants

Container grown plants have one major advantage over bareroot plants; they can be planted at any time of year, but planting in the late autumn makes them easiest to manage, giving them time to settle in before winter and ready to grow away strongly in the spring. Added to the garden in warmer months the plants will need regular watering, like any newly planted shrub or tree, to help them get established.

If you have the chance to select your plants, choose those with good growth, a well spaced framework of branches and avoid any plants that are pot bound or show any signs of pests or disease.

Above *This pot grown rhubarb is showing good growth and is ready for planting.*

Left *This container grown tree has been planted in a decorative terracotta pot for a year or two before being added to the garden.*

pruning

Feared and often over-complicated, pruning is the task most inexperienced gardeners feel least able to deal with. Although there are some very complex and exacting pruning methods required to grow trained trees or vines, for example, on the whole pruning is very simple, quickly done and a matter of common sense. It is perfectly possible to grow some fruit and never pick up a pair of secateurs. Some reassuring points to remember are:

- Pruning is much more straightforward when you are actually doing it than when you read about it in a book. It is one of those tasks where actually being shown what to do makes it child's play.
- If you get it wrong it probably will not matter in the long run, the very worst that may happen is the loss of one years harvest.
- If you don't prune one year you can almost certainly rectify things the next.
- There is a long window of opportunity to get most pruning done.
- You can grow fruit without ever pruning.

Right *Raspberries are very straightforward to prune. Old canes that have borne fruit are cut back to ground level.*

why prune?

The reasons for pruning are very basic: to keep a bush or tree a reasonable size to make harvesting and maintenance easier; to encourage greater yield and larger fruit; and to remove unfruitful growth. For bush and standard trees pruning during their first three or four years is the most important, as it establishes a good, robust framework of sturdy, well placed branches. If you buy well-established trees from a good nursery, this work will have been done already by experts and in most cases no further pruning is required. So, though more costly, it is worth buying established trees that have been well pruned if you can, as this is definitely the easiest option. Obviously you will be enjoying picking your own fruit much sooner, too.

The most exacting pruning tasks in the fruit garden are the trained trees, fans, espaliers, cordons, and step-over forms. During the first few years forming the shape requires patience, knowledge and a vision of how the framework will be formed. Then it is fairly time consuming and requires foresight to keep the shape developing in the right way and pruning has to be carried out twice a year at just the right time. Though beautiful, space saving and, in some cases, quite practical, these forms are not easy to maintain, so for an easy life stick to straightforward trees.

In many cases the term 'pruning' might be more reassuringly replaced with the less weighty 'cutting back'. Raspberries, blackberries, Japanese wineberries and the kiwi are all pruned by simply cutting back to ground level all growth that has fruited. What could be simpler?

Below *A pair of sharp secateurs make pruning quicker, easier and neater.*

no prune fruit

If you really want an easy life then there are fruitful plants that will produce happily without you having to wield the secateurs or loppers once a year.

- Blueberries
- Walnuts
- Sweet chestnuts
- Medlar
- Mulberries
- Strawberries (though they need cutting back it really can't be classed as pruning)
- Qunice
- Kiwi
- Cranberries
- Fig
- Damson
- Cape gooseberries
- Passion fruit
- Established plum and sweet cherry trees
- Established apple and pear trees

I have some magnificent old fruit trees in my town garden that have not been pruned in any way in the 15 years they have been in my care. I see them as part of the garden's structure and prefer them to look natural. Each spring they are covered in blossom and by late summer I have an abundance of apples. Only one has reverted to biennial fruiting, the Bramley's Seedling, which is to be expected. I am in no doubt though that the good pruning and shaping they received as young trees allows my neglect to be so fruitful.

Above *Strawberries are a 'no prune fruit' – old foliage just needs to be tidied and cut back.*

pruning strategy

Whatever you are tackling it helps if you take pruning each subject in four logical stages, standing back and assessing the plant after each:

- Cut out all dead, damaged or diseased wood.
- Cut out larger growth.
- Do any more detailed snipping back.
- Tidy up.

Step one can be termed remedial pruning, a technique that might be used on any garden shrub or tree to keep it healthy. At the right time of year remedial pruning can help keep even no prune trees in good shape.

pruning timetable

Most fruit trees and bushes are best pruned in the dormant period in the winter, and for some this window can be expanded to the autumn period after fruiting, so you can see there is really plenty of time to get it done. I tend to have a couple of blitz days: I pick a warm bright day when I want to be outside, muster all the tools I will need and work through the garden. In reality most things can be tackled at the same time if you wish. It is actually very satisfying to have a barrow full of prunings and a neat and tidy garden. The timetable here assumes the fruit is not grown in a restricted form.

autumn/winter

Sometime after the last fruit has been picked and before spring.

- Raspberry
- Autumn fruiting raspberry
- Japanese wineberry
- Blackberry
- Loganberry
- All hybrid berries

winter

- Apple
- Pear
- Fig
- Blackcurrant
- Redcurrant
- White currant
- Gooseberry
- Elderberry
- Grape
- Cob and filbert nuts

late winter /early spring

- Apricot
- Sour cherry

spring

- Peach
- Nectarine

midsummer

- Plum

late summer

- Cob and filbert nuts (brutting)

mulch

the annual mulch

Applying a good layer of organic mulch across the whole fruit garden is the cornerstone of maintaining the garden's fertility and literally feeding the soil, which will in turn feed your plants. It is a very simple task but makes growing fruit easier in many ways. Ideally the mulch will be a good mix of garden compost and farmyard manure spread at least three or four inches thick over the soil. The only exceptions are the acid loving fruits – blueberries and cranberries – as they prefer a mulch of pine needles, slightly rotted sawdust or seaweed.

why mulch?

Mulching makes the fruit garden easier to manage, the plants stronger and less likely to succumb to disease. The key benefits are:

- Weed suppression.
- Moisture conservation.
- Reducing soil erosion and loss of fertility from extreme weather conditions.
- Adding nutrients.
- Improving soil structure and adding bulk.
- Warming the soil in winter and cooling in summer.

Below *A good coating of grass clippings around these young blackcurrant bushes will protect them from weeds and help maintain moisture levels in the soil.*

The mulch not only improves the fertility of the soil, it will improve the soil's texture, aid drainage, stop water loss and suppress weed growth. It is amazing how the rich material is eagerly pulled down into the soil by worms.

The soil should be damp and weed-free before you spread the mulch and avoid mulching on days when the soil is frozen. You can pile the mulch onto the beds using a spade or fork, although it is easier to shovel the compost into a rubber garden tub, then hold the two handles together and use it like a jug to tip the mulch between plants. A hoe or rake can be useful for spreading the mulch around once it is on the soil.

There is an argument for mulching in spring – the nutrient value of the mulch can be washed away during the winter, whereas apply in the spring and the plants are ready to come to life and take advantage of the feed. However, applied in the autumn the mulch protects the soil through the winter. I tend to apply mine in late winter/early spring as part of the garden tidy up and reawakening, but tucking the plants up for winter has its advantages. In reality the beds in my fruit garden are seldom without some kind of covering such as grass cuttings, leafmould paper or a mat of companion plants to protect the soil.

garden compost and other mulches

Use to describe anything that is used to cover the surface of the soil, a mulch can be organic or inorganic. Mulch is quick and simple to spread on to the garden and boasts a long list of benefits. Many materials you might use as mulch are free and, in fact, it is an easy way to dispose of garden waste such as grass clippings. A good covering of any mulch will suppress weed growth, help retain moisture in the soil and protect the surface of the soil from erosion. Beyond that organic mulch will add bulk and improve the texture of the soil, aid drainage and, to varying degrees, improve soil fertility as the material breaks down and is pulled down into the soil by worms. In a soil that is really 'alive' with plenty of worms and micro organisms, it is amazing how quickly a layer of mulch is processed.

the rules

- Apply to damp soil when there is no ground frost.
- Apply a layer about 7.5–10 cm (3–4 in) thick – any less will not be effective.
- Leave a 5 cm (2 in) gap around the trunk of fruit trees, bushes and the crowns of rhubarb and strawberry plants.

I apply a good layer of a mix of garden compost and farmyard manure in the late winter or early spring in what I call my annual mulch. This is the basic method by which I return fertility to the soil. At other times of the year I spread grass clippings on the fruit beds in rotation as the lawn is mown and, when it is available, add a good layer of leafmould, too. All materials that cost nothing and really work wonders. The only inorganic mulch I use is a weed-suppressing membrane on the strawberry bed. This keeps the weeds down, the fruit clean and stops the terrible tangle created when runners root before I have got around to removing them. If annual weeds are getting out of hand amongst vulnerable plants, covering the bed with a layer of newspaper then piling a hefty layer of grass clippings or other mulch on top should kill most, but I would not rely on this method for pernicious perennial weeds such as ground elder or horsetail.

If you are mulching around small, lone trees or bushes, apply mulch to the extent of its canopy.

top fruit garden mulches

seaweed

Used as a mulch, seaweed adds a fantastic range of trace elements to the soil and is rich in nitrogen and potash. It is best applied in a thick layer in the late autumn/early winter – used at the hotter times of the year it smells terrible and attracts hosts of flies.

It is worth checking the regulations regarding the collection of seaweed in your area before gathering up a sack load.

grass clippings

Disposing of grass clippings for anyone with a fair-sized lawn can be tricky. Too thick a layer on the compost heap results in a black slime, so using a few hopper loads around the fruit bushes in rotation is an easy and useful method of disposing of them.

straw

For most of us this is bought-in mulch. It is quick and clean to get onto the soil and a good layer will keep down weeds and warm the soil. The straw rots very slowly and a good layer should last all season. It is often used around strawberry plants because it also keeps the fruit clean, but can be equally valuable around other fruiting plants, though it has little nutrient value. The only down side is it can travel around the garden a little and birds find it attractive to forage in. Scattering it widely but watering well when it first goes down can help it to stay put.

mushroom compost

A by-product of the mushroom growing industry, mushroom compost's contribution to the soil's fertility is reasonable, but it is great for adding bulk to the soil and improving the soil's texture. This compost often has a high pH, so it should not be used around acid-loving plants.

wood ash

Wood ash is especially good for fruiting plants as it contains high levels of potash. Only use ash that you can be sure no plastics or materials are likely to have contaminated the ash.

Above right *Seaweed is a useful mulch, especially (if local regulations allow) if it can be gathered for free.*

Right *A good layer of grass clippings around rhubarb helps maintain the moisture levels in the soil, but avoid getting mulch on the crown.*

Left *Well-rotted stable manure can often be obtained from riding stables who will be only too pleased to be rid of it, though you will probably have to bag it yourself.*

Right *These dry brown leaves, given the right conditions and one or two years, will become one of the finest soil conditioners.*

farmyard manure

Manure must be well-rotted before it is spread on the garden – this means it must be 6 to 12 months old. The exact nature of the manure will vary according to the bedding that has been used, but it is a brilliant soil conditioner and gives good dose of nutrients vital to growing good fruit. On heavy clay soils it opens up the soil and aids drainage, and on lighter soils manure will bind the soil together, helping it to hold onto moisture. It is available from garden centres in neatly packaged sacks, but this is an expensive option. Many farms and riding stables will let you have manure for nothing if you fill your own sacks.

newspaper, cardboard and purpose-made paper mulch

Paper or card protects the surface of the soil and keeps weeds down. The downside is that it doesn't look very attractive. To be successful, the paper must be a several sheets thick and overlapped (central fold to central fold if possible) as the edges need to be tucked well into the soil and it may be necessary to anchor the paper with large stones or bricks. Purpose-made rolls of organic paper mulch are available, and they are usually a less obtrusive plain brown.

leafmould

Easy to make and completely free, leafmould is a brilliant soil conditioner. Well-rotted leafmould, crumbly and brown, really looks like it is full of organic goodness, but in truth it contains much lower levels of nutrients than manure or garden compost. However, it is fantastic for improving the texture of the soil and beds look very smart with a new layer of dark leafmould.

Most of us have to sweep or vacuum autumn leaves from driveways or lawns and it is child's play to convert these leaves into leafmould. If your patch is a bit short on this particular autumn treasure then there are still plenty of non-gardeners who will probably be delighted to be rid of their fallen leaves. Simply pile the leaves into black bin liners, tie them up, stab to create a few holes and dump them behind a shed or under a large shrub to rot for a year or two. Alternatively if you have the space, construct a large bin from posts knocked into the ground in a square with chicken wire wrapped around them. After some building work I have started using the large cubic metre delivery bags sand and gravel often come in, filling them about three quarters full and turning in the top. Many leaf vacuums chew up the leaves as they are collected which hastens the process. Tipping a heap of leaves on the lawn and running over them with the lawn mower has a similar effect.

For a real shortcut the fallen leaves can be dumped straight onto the soil, where they will protect the soil from the worst of the winter weather and rot down in situ.

pine needles

Like leafmould, pine needles have little nutritional value but are a great soil conditioner for use around acid-loving blueberries and cranberries.

green or living mulches

Any plant that cover the soil with a protective green canopy could be described as a green mulch. Trailing nasturtiums used as companion plants usually perform this role if planted thickly enough. Even a covering of weeds gives the same benefit in protecting the soil, and some will actually help make nutrients available to the plants in the bed. The term is more usually used to describe a plant deliberately sown to provide a dense mat of growth that protects the soil, and once dug into the soil boosts fertility. Winter tares, grazing rye, field beans and forage peas are all popular choices.

Above left *Under most pines you will find a thick layer of fallen needles. Scrape away the top layer and the needles below will be brown and beginning to decay. This material makes the perfect mulch for acid-loving blueberries and cranberries.*

Above *If you are desperate to eradicate established weeds under fruit bushes, lay weed-suppressing membrane and cover with bark chips to dress it up, then wait a year before removing and applying a good layer of compost.*

garden compost

Compost is not as high in nutrients as farmyard manure, but it adds bulk and a good dose of humus to the soil, which means moisture and nutrients can be retained in the soil more effectively. There are a multitude of methods of producing compost – the traditional large timber bins, smaller dustbin-sized plastic bins or small composting wormeries – so everyone should be able to produce at least some compost. It is possible to buy garden compost, but if you can it is well worth making your own, as it takes little effort and recycles garden and household waste into something incredibly valuable for the fruit plot. Beware other people's compost. If they haven't strictly observed the 'what not to compost' advice you could be spreading weeds and disease as you mulch.

what to compost

- Grass clippings.
- Garden waste.
- Kitchen waste such as egg shells and vegetable peelings.
- Shredded bark and prunings.
- Newspaper, card and egg boxes.
- Tea bags and coffee grounds.
- Leaves.
- Weed tops (no flowers or seed heads).
- Animal manure.

what not to compost

- Plants treated with herbicide.
- Diseased plants.
- Weeds that have gone to seed or the roots of pernicious weeds.
- Cooked food waste and dairy products.
- Woody material, unless it has been shredded.

Left *Encourage good composting habits by keeping a bucket for vegetable peelings in the kitchen.*

making compost

- Add equal quantities of lush green and fibrous brown material to your heap.
- Alternate layers of green and brown material a few inches thick.
- Add a covering to regulate moisture and keep in heat.
- If it is too wet and slimy, mix in shredded paper, card or coarse material.
- If it is slow to rot down add farmyard manure.
- If it is too dry add water and ensure your cover is effective.
- Don't expect perfection – your compost will be lumpy and uneven. Some tougher stems and stalks may not rot the first time round.
- Generally just keep adding material and leave the micro fauna to do their work.

The key to making good compost is having a good mix of wet, lush, green, nitrogen-rich material, like grass clipping and more fibrous, dry, brown, carbon-rich material like shredded bark and shredded newspaper. The composting process is down to the work of micro-organisms and fungi, and to work efficiently they need air, nitrogen, warmth and moisture. The composting process produces heat which should kill most weed seeds and diseases, but there is no guaranteeing these high temperatures will be reached or sustained, so I recommend never knowingly composting diseased growth or weeds that have gone to seed. About a cubic metre/yard of material is required to generate enough heat for the composting process to really get going, but a larger heap will be more effective. If you have the space then it pays to have three compost bins; this allows for one bin being filled, one maturing and one being used on the garden.

Left *Four old pallets lashed together make a perfectly adequate compost bin, big enough to hold sufficient material for the heap to work well.*

Above right *These hard-working worms are what transforms the waste in the wormery into black gold.*

composting wormery

If space is limited, a worm compost bin may be a good choice. These are large plastic bins in which worms digest the organic material you add and the resulting compost is composed of very fertile worm casts. The advantage is not just that the bin itself is compact, but you can compost kitchen waste that cannot be put on the regular compost heap. Many gardeners have compost heaps and a wormery. Start the worm bin with a layer of garden compost or manure and the worms, on top of some shredded newspaper and some crocks or gravel for drainage. Normally brandling or tiger worms are used, and these can be easily bought on-line. Keep adding kitchen waste and use a layer of newspaper as a cover. There is a tap at the bottom of wormeries so the liquid produced can be drained off. This is a valuable liquid fertilizer which must be diluted before being used on the garden. This is especially useful if you are growing fruit in containers. When the compost is ready for use, spread it around your fruit plants after sieving out enough worms to produce your next batch.

watering

Keeping the fruit trees and bushes in your garden watered need not be a chore, especially if you know when and how to water. Many gardeners water when in fact there is no need.

Fruit trees or bushes need the most careful watering in the first season after planting. Bareroot and container grown plants added to the garden in early autumn soon after leaf fall should be the easiest to manage. They will look after themselves until growth begins and then should be well enough established to be watered liberally once a week, if the weather requires. Container grown plants added to the garden in spring or even summer will need more careful monitoring and may need watering more frequently, possibly once a day until settled in.

Once established, plants will only require watering in extremely dry periods. For the most part healthy plants with a good root system should be capable of fending for themselves except when rainfall is very limited, then it is better to soak plants once a week rather than watering little and often. The most important time for fruiting plants to have sufficient water is while the fruit is swelling, from the fruit setting until harvest.

The need for irrigation can be reduced by applying a good wodge of mulch. Keeping the surface of the soil covered in mulch reduces the evaporation of water from the soil and ensuring the soil contains plenty of organic matter will make it better at retaining moisture.

Even with the right soil and mulch there are times when watering is essential. The task can be made easier by using a variety of irrigation equipment. The need for watering in the fruit garden is most likely to be sporadic and only particularly demanding in the first year, except in very warm areas. For this reason installing a simple irrigation system, as you might in the veg patch, is really unnecessary. The easiest option is to use a seep hose or a number of seep hoses. These are a very efficient way of getting the water to plants. The hoses lay on the surface of the soil coiled around the plants and meandering wherever water is required. Water flows through the hose and literally seeps out along its length. If a bed is newly planted I leave a seep hose in place for the first year, shuffled under the mulch. Otherwise I move them around the garden as needed. The attachment at the end of the seep hose should fit snugly into the regular hose. The pump or tap could even be fitted with an automatic timer for real ease.

It is worth pointing out it is not just pure laziness that dictates watering is kept to a minimum. Water is obviously a valuable resource and over-watering can have a detrimental effect, leaching nutrients from the soil and causing erosion.

Right *Vintage watering cans are practical and look decorative when left around the garden.*

weeding

Any plant growing where it is not wanted is a weed. Many gardeners strive to keep their patch as weed-free as possible, as weeds steal light, nutrients and moisture from the plants you are nurturing. There are many strategies available to wage war on weeds; the chemical quick fix is not one I use (especially around fruit). I prefer to rely on hoeing, mulching and a good blitz now and again to keep the weeds down. I also try to keep a healthy perspective on just how much damage weeds are actually doing my fruit, knowing when to act quickly, when I can turn a blind eye and when the weeds might actually be doing me a favour.

when weeds are good

There is a strong argument for not weeding in some circumstances; in fact it is just possible that the weeds are doing more good than harm. A layer of weeds is in effect a green mulch, protecting the soil from erosion and moisture loss. Weeds with taproots can help to break up heavy soil, and some will provide a home and food for beneficial insects. But perhaps the most potentially valuable of all are those that actually increase the fertility of the soil. These are the nitrogen fixers, like clover, that have a symbiotic relationship with bacteria in the soil, such that they can absorb nitrogen from the air and store it in their roots.

The other group are known as dynamic accumulators. These are plants that are known to bring up nutrients from deep in the soil, making them available to other plants. Dandelions and nettles are amongst the best dynamic accumulators. Others are dock, meadow sweet and coltsfoot. Using dynamic accumulators to improve fertility is a common feature of permaculture guilds, and a consideration in some companion planting (see pages 199–200). There is a strong argument for leaving these weeds be, at least in some areas, and cutting them to the ground before they set seed, using the lush green growth to fire-up the compost heap. You might do this a few times a year.

prevention is better than weeding

There are times when keeping soil weed-free might be required; if plants are young and just getting established, if you wish to use your own companion or under-planting, rather than a serendipitous one nature provides, or if you just want a weed-free patch. Prevention or early action is much more effective than waiting until things are completely out of hand. The simplest route is a regular application of mulch. The annual mulch will go a long way to keeping weeds down, but further applications of organic matter will help. Each of my beds receives a good layer of grass clippings, probably twice in the season, in rotation. Biodegradable paper mulch (newspaper or specifically designed for the job), put down early in the year, should keep a bed weed-free for the whole season, and then just rot away into the soil. A more aggressive route is to mulch the bed with a polythene sheet or a weed-suppressing membrane. This will keep weeds at bay for several years but also means you cannot easily work on the soil's fertility, except with liquid feeds. I only use this method on strawberry beds where it has significant advantages and I know the planting will only be for three or four years.

Hoeing is another form of weed prevention, as it is at its most effective when weed seedlings are yet to appear above the soils surface. Shallow hoeing slices the plants growing tip off before it can appear above ground. Hoeing also has the advantage of leaving the soil structure mostly intact and not disturbing the roots of shallow rooted plants. If weeds are already through the soil hoeing can still be used, but it is best done on a warm day when the sun can be relied upon to shrivel their remains before the weeds are able to re-root.

natural defences

A healthy garden is one where plants are grown to be robust, with a living soil, a buzzing insect population, small mammals, amphibians and a wide diversity of plants. A garden like this is best equipped to shrug off attacks from insects, pests and diseases. In this kind of garden biodiversity is nurtured, and nature's checks and balances will be at work. Companion planting and encouraging beneficial species into the garden can make fruit growing easier. Beyond these practicalities, walking out into a garden alive with insects, with an abundance of colour, texture and variety, and full of birdsong, is truly uplifting. Working with nature is easier than battling with it.

natural predators

These are the gardener's allies, wildlife that will work for the garden protecting plants from damage by consuming hoards of pests. Recruiting these voracious predators into the garden is simple and once they are around pest control becomes a great deal easier.

ground beetles

Eat insect larvae and insect eggs. Encourage them by leaving some areas of rough grass and keeping the soil well covered.

centipedes

Feed on small insects and slugs. As with the ground beetle, they can be encouraged with good ground cover.

hoverflies

Not to be mistaken for their plumper wasp lookalikes, hoverflies lay their eggs in aphid colonies and when the larvae hatch they consume vast numbers of aphids. Attract the hoverflies in to protect your fruit by planting tagetes, nasturtiums and calendula.

ladybirds

Both the adult and the larvae consume aphids rapaciously. Providing suitable habitats for overwintering will help swell the population of ladybirds. Dry bundles of canes and sticks crammed into a terracotta pot and put in a sheltered spot should do the trick.

lacewings

Another avid aphid predator, lacewings are not specifically attracted by flowers but will appreciate the snug overwintering quarters described for ladybirds

bees

As a beekeeper I cannot help mentioning the fantastic job done by honey bees in ensuring flowers are successfully pollinated. If you see them working in your garden be grateful and treat them with respect.

birds

Consuming slugs, aphids, caterpillars and larvae, birds are really the fruit gardener's friend when they are not stealing the fruit! Net fruit securely and leave them to eat the things you want less of.

frogs and toads

Eat slugs and small insects – the tiniest pond will encourage them to breed in the garden but cool, hidden micro-habitats in a log pile, for instance, will give them somewhere to hide away.

hedgehogs

Bumbling and shy, these prickly characters are a gardener's friend, consuming slugs, woodlice, millipedes and wireworms. Encourage them by providing log piles in sheltered, uncultivated areas.

Right *The cute, fairytale appearance of the ladybird belies its true character as one of the gardener's greatest allies in the battle against aphids.*

companion planting

An incredibly valuable tool in making your fruit garden easier to manage, companion planting is the technique of growing other plants alongside fruit trees and bushes to make them more fruitful or more straightforward to care for. Many suggested planting combinations are drawn from observation and common sense, some now have a scientific basis and some are perhaps more folk lore than fact. However even those not rooted in scientific fact might be worth a try and at the very least they will make the fruit garden a more colourful place and prevent areas becoming an unhealthy monoculture.

A companion plant might do one or more of the following: provide food or shelter for natural pest predators, produce chemicals to deter pests, prevent weed growth or provide nutrients. The term could even be applied to using a shelter belt of poplar or damson trees to protect an orchard from frost or wind damage.

Not only of can using companion plants make your fruit garden healthier and easier to maintain, they can also bring colour, fragrance, volume and life. Some companion plants are a permanent part of my fruit garden's design. My beds are set in a formal pattern and I line the long beds with strips of chives – a great companion plant with pretty flowers – while the central path is lined with lavender (great for attracting pollinators). Each is a permanent and important part of the garden's design. In early summer I cram the beds planted with fruit bushes with trailing nasturtiums, French marigolds and calendula – easy-going plants that flower copiously until the first frosts. They act as living mulch, protecting the soil from erosion, smothering weeds as well as attracting pollinators and predators. The marigolds produce a chemical called thiopene that deters nematodes. The nasturtiums and the calendula flowers are edible so they really earn their place in the garden. Though there are masses of proven, traditional companion plants, most nectar-rich plants will be of use in attracting pollenators to fruit bushes.

Left *Early in the summer these wonderful companion plants are already earning their keep. The flowers of calendula and nasturtiums, and fragrant blue lavender, all make excellent companion plants.*

good companions

Here is a list of popular companion plants and the influence they have or are reputed to have.

- **Alliums & fruit trees**
  Repel aphids and fruit tree borers.
- **Borage & strawberries & fruit trees**
  Adds potassium, calcium and other minerals.
- **Hyssop & grapes**
  Reputed to help growth.
- **Marigolds or tagetes**
  Repel harmful nematodes in the soil.
- **Nasturtiums & fruit trees, strawberries & general**
  Repels fruit borers, trap crop for aphids.
- **Tansy & raspberries & black berries**
  Repels flying insects.

Above *The French marigold is striking, adding a shock of colour, as well as being a useful companion plant.*

Right *The beautiful flowers of the nasturtium lure beneficial insects into the fruit garden.*

If you are adding companion plants to the garden they really should be no trouble at all. I find nasturtiums are one of the best. Push the seed into the ground in the spring and they should flower continuously through to the first frost with no care at all. Best of all they will normally self seed, so you only need to plant them once. If conditions really suit them they can get a little out of hand, but hacking them back takes seconds and they will just throw up a host of new leaves.

pests and diseases

The best defence you can have against any pest or disease is to grow strong healthy plants. This starts with buying plants from reputable suppliers whose plants are disease-free and have been cared for well before they get to you. Plant them well, in healthy living soil with plenty of organic matter at the right level. Water newly planted trees and bushes until they are established so they do not become stressed. Plants that have been grown well have the best chance of shirking off a pest or disease attack without any lasting damage and getting on with producing fruit. Any plant that is under attack can be given a boost with a foliar spray of seaweed solution to help it triumph. If you have a persistent problem, replace existing plants with resistant varieties in another part of the garden.

Inevitably, however, some infestations or health problems will need intervention or at the least an understanding of what conditions might predispose plants to certain problems so these can be modified. When removing diseased growth, clean all pruning tools thoroughly and destroy diseased fruit, leaves and wood. Never compost diseased material.

pests

birds

Agile, daring and relentless, birds are undoubtedly the pest most likely to ravage your fruit crop. They do favour some fruits more than others – blueberries, strawberries, redcurrants, cherries and raspberries are favourites – but any crop might come under attack. They will happily strip plants of fruit which is far from ripe. Moving, shining objects designed to scare them away may work for a while, but they will soon become habituated to these strategies, especially if the lure is great enough.

The only real solution is to keep the birds away from the fruit, and I mean right away, as they will happily perch on your defences and peck through to the fruit. Covers need to be in place well before the fruit is ripe. Growing all your fruit in a permanent fruit cage is the best protection, however this is not always possible. Fruit cages are a significant investment and only work where all your fruit is in a confined area.

I favour fortifying beds of fruit as necessary. I rely on temporary structures of nets, chicken wire and canes which I can move around the garden as needed. On the wire supports I simply fling a length of mesh over the top and anchor it at the base, ensuring it is pulled well away from the fruit. The ends can be tied with twine or wire. Traditional fruit nets are thick threads knotted together much like fishing net. I would urge against using this type of net as birds easily become tangled. The more robust square plastic mesh is less of a hazard to the birds and is easier to handle. Chicken wire also makes a stout temporary enclosure. However you rig your barricades you will need access to pick the fruit yourself, so leave an easily opened gap or allow for the netting to be rolled up for harvesting.

Birds can cause damage at other times of year. Bullfinches and sparrows in particular can peck out the centre of buds in late winter and early spring. Cherries, pears and plums are the biggest targets. Large trees are impossible to net, but should be prolific enough to produce a good crop in spite of the damage. Smaller, young trees can be protected by netting.

At other times of the year birds are valuable allies in the garden, clearing up the larvae of many other pests and aphids, so be sure to take nets away once all the fruit has been picked.

wasps

Wasps not only spoil your fruit, they can be a real nuisance too, limiting your enjoyment of the garden. The first, simple step to attracting fewer wasps into the garden is to regularly pick up all fallen fruit.

Damaged fruit rotting on the ground is perfect wasp bait. With this in mind take care when picking up windfalls as wasps are bad tempered when disturbed. Secondly, protect your fruit from the birds. Wasps seldom start the process, they merely exploit damage done by others, so protecting your fruit from bird damage will go a long way to keeping down the number of wasps. If numbers become intolerable, glass wasp traps will help.

aphids

Aphids may be small but the effects that a growing population can have on a plant can be immense. As in other parts of the garden aphids suck the sap of the plant from young shoots, and this can result in stunted, deformed growth. They transmit virus diseases and the sooty mould grows on the honeydew the aphids exude. There are a number of aphids specifically adapted to living on the plants in the fruit garden, including the currant blister aphid and the gooseberry aphid. In a healthy garden with plenty of predators the problem should be lessened, as ladybird larvae and hoverflies will consume hoards of aphids. However, once an infestation takes hold the population will multiply quickly. Ants contribute to the problem as they 'farm' the aphids and can protect them from predation. The simplest approach is to deal with the problem quickly before numbers become too great and simply wipe the aphids from the plant or dislodge them with a powerful jet of water. If the population gets out of hand then use a soapy water spray.

diseases

brown rot

Affects Apples, pears, plums, cherries, nectarines, peaches, apricots.
Signs Fruit becomes brown and rots on the trees, as it progresses concentric rings of cream coloured pustules can appear. In the spring the same infection causes blossom to wilt and turn brown.
Cause A fungal infection attacks fruit already damaged by birds, wasps or coddling moth.
Solution Remove damaged fruit to prevent infection and protect fruit from damage.

codling moth

Affects Apples, pears and plums.
Signs Outwardly the fruit may look fine but rather alarmingly once the fruit is cut open (or worse still bitten into) the centre of the fruit is brown and rotten and a creamy-coloured maggot may still be present.
Cause The eggs of the female coddling moth hatch and the tiny maggots bore into the fruit.
Solution There is a nematode called sleinernema carpocapsae that can be sprayed onto the tree in the early autumn and will kill the maggots, thus lessening the population for the following year. However, this doesn't stop new moths flying into your garden next year. The other option is to use a pheromone trap to lure in moths before the eggs are laid. This may have some impact on the population.

scab

Affects Apples and pears.
Signs Scabby-type pits on the fruit which may become distorted and crack. The shoots and leaves can also be affected – the leaves have spots and may drop prematurely while shoots can become split and damaged. This damage can in turn allow in other infections.
Causes One of two similar fungal diseases.
Solutions Destroy all affected material to limit the spread of the fungal spores. However the spores will travel miles.
Resistant cultivars: Apples – Beauty of Bath, Brown Lees Russet, Discovery, Lane's Prince Albert, Tom Putt, Wheeler's Russet, Red Devil; Pears – Beurre Hardy, Hessle, Jargonelle, Black Worcester.

silver leaf

Affects Plums are particularly susceptible but cherries, almonds, apricots and apples can be affected.
Signs The surface of the leaf takes on a silver appearance, turns brown and eventually the branch will die. The discolouration of the leaves can be confused with what is called false silver leaf, caused by some form of stress, cold or lack of water. When a branch affected by genuine silver leaf is cut it has irregular dark patches of damage running through it, while its imitator does not.

Causes A fungal infection that enters through wounds to the bark of the tree.
Solutions Prune particularly susceptible trees in the summer when there are less spores and the tree will heal more quickly. Remove all affected wood to a point about 15 cm (6 in) beyond the infected wood.

bacterial canker

Affects Stone fruit.
Symptoms: Sunken areas in the bark of the tree, probably with a nasty looking sticky substance. The leaves also develop small holes in them, referred to as shot holes. These could easily be mistaken for caterpillar damage.
Cause One of a number of bacteria, the problem is more prevalent in very wet autumns and springs.
Solution Quick action is needed to stop the disease. Cut out all affected wood about 15 cm (6 in) into healthy wood and paint the wounds with tree wound seal. Burn all the diseased material. To help prevent infections prune in the summer.
Resistant Cultivars Plum – Marjorie's seedling, Cherries, Merton Glory, Merton Premier.

fungal canker

Affects Apples, pears and mulberries.
Symptoms Sunken areas in the bark of the tree. Badly affected growth may die back completely. Affected fruit does not ripen.
Cause Fungal infection entering the tree through wounds or damage.
Solution If possible remove the affected branch or spur entirely. Paint wounds with a wound sealant. On the trunk scrape away the infected material to clean wood to stop the infection spreading. Spray with Bordeaux mix. Improving drainage can help.
Resistant Cultivars Apples – Spartan, Laxton's Superb, Bramley Seedling, Lane's Prince Albert.

Left *The wound that probably allowed the fungal infection brown rot to attack this pear is clearly visible.*

botrytis

Affected Many, though you are most likely to see this problem on strawberries and other soft fruit.
Symptoms Fluffy, grey/white fungal growth.
Causes An airborne fungus, which is just about everywhere, it can be spread in water, in the air and persists in the soil from year to year.
Solutions Remove all affected fruit or growth as soon as you see it. Keeping things spick and span is the best defence as the fungus is so widespread. Clear away over-ripe fruit and damaged stems. Leaving over-ripe soft fruit on the plant to rot can lead to botrytis, so timely harvesting is wise.

fruit garden timetable

It is impossible to give hard and fast rules about when some tasks should be done as so much depends on the vagaries of the weather. Winter can drag its heals or spring can arrive early, and late frosts can surprise us all. So while the tasks are divided loosely by season and into early and late within the season, common sense should always prevail.

early spring

- Apply an all purpose organic fertilizer and mulch with well-rotted manure or garden compost (or a mix of the two) around fruit trees, bushes and canes.
- Prune fan-trained nectarines, peaches and apricots.
- Finish any remaining planting.
- Protect early blossom from frosts.
- Pick forced rhubarb.

late spring

- Protect blossom from late frosts.
- Start looking out for gooseberry saw fly.
- Water newly-planted bushes and trees if the weather is dry.
- If strawberries are grown without a sheet mulch, mulch with straw.
- Put out codling moth traps.
- Move container grown fig trees outside once the risk of frosts has passed.
- Pick rhubarb.

early summer

- Tie in new growth of cane fruit.
- Chop off strawberry runners.
- Water newly planted bushes and trees.
- Expect fruit trees to shed some of the fruit that has set.
- Thin tree fruits if desired (after trees have shed some of the crop).
- Thin grapes, snipping off about one in two or three grapes, if desired.
- Pinch out growing tips of fig trees.
- Protect soft fruit and cherries from the birds well before they ripen.
- Pick strawberries, raspberries, black, red and white currants, gooseberries for cooking, Japanese wineberries.

late summer

- Tie in new growth of fruit canes.
- Train and tie in fan trained trees.
- Plant new strawberry beds.
- Prune peaches and nectarines.
- Prune plums and Damson if necessary.
- Prune fan-trained sour cherries and restricted forms of apples and pears.
- Start planning any new planting schemes.
- Order bareroot bushes and trees.
- Start soil preparation and building (if required) of new planting areas.
- Pick strawberries, dessert gooseberries, blackberries, raspberries, cherries, grapes, early apples, plums, Damson, kiwi, figs and melons.

early autumn

- Order bareroot trees and bushes.
- Continue soil preparation and building.
- Pick apples, pears, blackberries, autumn fruiting raspberries and strawberries (perpetual).

late autumn

- Prune autumn fruiting raspberries, cut them to the ground.
- Finish pruning raspberries, blackberries and Japanese wineberries.
- Begin planting bareroot plants as soon as they are available, as soon as all leaves are fallen.
- The best time to plant container grown plants.
- Check tree stakes and ties before the harsh weather begins.
- Put grease bands on trees.

early winter

- Prune apples and pears if necessary.
- Continue planting when the weather is suitable.
- Move container grown figs to a frost-free location, or wrap trees in fleece.
- Wrap pots in hessian or bubble wrap if you expect severe frosts.

late winter

- On fine days finish off planting and pruning if needed.
- Prune autumn fruiting raspberries.

storing fruit

Once your fruit garden is well established you will undoubtedly be in the fortunate position of having a glut. Giving fruit fresh from the garden to friends and family is obviously rewarding, but it is worth knowing how to squirrel away some of your harvest to enjoy in the long, chilly days of winter. With a glut comes guilt, watching the fruit you have craved rot under the tree because you just haven't had a moment to pick it is not a rarity among gardeners. Remembering, at the very least, your neglected fruit will be feeding birds and insects at a challenging time of year helps.

In times gone by stacking away every bit of potential food was a necessity and storage had to take the form of preserves or drying. Now we have a much simpler convenient form of preservation – freezing – although it is very satisfying to have a pantry shelf lined with homemade preserves to see you through the winter. There are a number of ways of storing or preserving fruit, some more time consuming than others. Freezing is the simplest option, whilst processing the fruit to make jam, chutney, wine or cider is more complex and an art in itself.

freezing

This is the easiest, quickest way to preserve fruit and leaves you with the freedom to choose exactly how to use it later. The good news is that fruit frozen promptly and efficiently retains its nutritional value and taste, though it will darken in colour and become soft when defrosted. Some fruits hold up better than others. Soft fruit can collapse and strawberries turn to mush, but they still taste great and are fine for use in cooking.

For berries, spread the clean ripe berries in a single layer on a tray and put them in the freezer. As soon as they are frozen pack the berries into bags or plastic storage boxes, remove as much air as possible, seal and label. Bags or boxes used in the freezer should be moisture-proof. This way the berries should retain as much shape as possible and allow you to remove a handful or two from the box as required rather than a large lump. For apples and pears, peel and core the fruit before freezing. Even melon and grapes can be frozen reasonably successfully.

Creating a purée or stewing fruit before it is frozen is another option, ideal for throwing together a quick pie or crumble. A childhood favourite was my mother's raspberry jam (more of a thick sauce that was stored in the freezer), its rich jewel-like colour and shine looked and tasted great on ice cream and steamed puddings.

cool storing

If you have a cool shed, garage, cellar or spare room then apples, and to some extent pears, can be stored just as they are picked, without processing. Generally only apples which ripen late in the season can be stored. Mid-season apples might store for a few weeks, later cultivars will keep for up to six months depending on the conditions and variety. Fruit should be laid out on trays or in boxes with space between them. The trays or boxes can be stacked so long as air can move freely around them. Attractive wooden storage shelves are available, they look like a very open chest of drawers where the base of the draws is narrow wooden slats. The basic principles of this method are to keep the fruits cool, with air circulating between them, and to prevent the fruits from touching each other so one rotting fruit wont damage the rest of the crop. An alternative, easier method is to put a number of apples in a plastic bag, turn the top down, puncture a few holes in the bag and place the bags in a cool, dry, dark place. It is only worth trying to store perfect unblemished fruit.

Most of us are used to year round 'supermarket perfect' apples, but the reality of home storing is slightly different. After a time the skin of most apples will wither and the flesh become softer. This is fine if you are cooking with the apples but they will not be as appealing to eat raw. Pears do not store as well as apples and deteriorate quickly so need checking regularly.

the best keepers

Dessert Apples

Elstar Delicious flavour retained well on keeping, crisp texture with a red flushed skin, very productive. Keeps for three months.

Fiesta A red apple with an aromatic flavour. Keeps for six months.

Tydeman's Late Orange A Cox's Orange Pippin type apple but a much better keeper, easy to grow. Keeps for 6 months.

Blenheim Orange Can also be used for cooking. Crisp texture with a nutty taste. Keeps for five months.

Cooking apples

Bountiful A sweet cooker produced on a small tree. Keeps for about three months.

Bramley's apple seedling Very popular large cooker but it is a large tree and has a tendency to produce biennially. Keeps for about five months.

Edward VII A very late, hardy variety. Its late ripening and good keeping qualities mean you should be enjoying this apple right through to the following spring. Keeps for about six months.

Above *Cox's Orange Pippin is not known for its great keeping qualities so best to enjoy the fruit once it is ripe.*

combining fruit with alcohol

Steeping fruit in vodka, gin or brandy in the late summer or early autumn will create a warming liqueur that will be ready for drinking on chilly winter evenings. The exact proportions are, to some extent, a matter of taste, and each can be made sweeter by adding a touch more sugar at the occasional tasting to check progress. Simply put the fruit, alcohol and sugar in a stoppered bottle or airtight jar (making it in a bottle is a little laborious as the berries have to be popped in one at a time), put it in a cool dark place, shake gently every few days until the sugar dissolves, then leave to mature. All need to be kept for at least two or three months before drinking and all will improve with age.

raspberry vodka

300 g (11 oz) raspberries
350 g (12 oz) caster sugar
1.5 litres (2½ pints) vodka

sloe gin

450 g (1 lb) sloes
225 g (8 oz) caster sugar
1 litre (1¾ pints) gin

bramble brandy

450 g (1 lb) blackberries
225 g (8 oz) caster sugar
1 litre (1¾ pints) brandy

jams and chutneys

Jams are simple to make once you know the basics. Chutneys can be more laborious with long lists of ingredients to muster, but have the advantage over jams that over-ripe fruit can make good chutney whilst it will not make good jam. In my constant pursuit of time saving methods I always feel it is better to make a big batch of jam than a smaller one; it takes just the same amount of effort as making a smaller batch but you end up with more lovely jars of jam on the pantry shelf. This means I often combine fruits to make what I consider a worthwhile batch, the tail end of one crop with the start of another, perhaps.

Above *Raspberries make tasty jam and can be used to flavour spirits.*

Right *Opening a cupboard or pantry crammed with preserves made from delicious, home-grown fruit is immensely satisfying.*

tools

keep it simple

The garden tasks for the average fruit gardener are few and simple, so it follows that the tools required are few and simple too. There are plenty of tempting gadgets and tools in all sizes and colours on the market, but life and storage is far more straightforward if you keep just the minimum number of basic tools. Do invest in stout, sturdy tools if you can. Second hand or junk shops often have older tools that are very well made and serviceable. If you have a tendency to abandon your tools in the garden for days at a time go for plastic handles, which will not rot as wood does.

hoe

A flat-bladed dutch hoe is best for clearing weed seedlings from around shallow rooted fruit bushes.

trowel

Used for planting and weeding. Trowels are easily lost, many have wooden handles and even a green painted metal blade making them perfectly camouflaged when left amongst on the soil around leafy plants. Consequently I recommend purchasing two or three stout but inexpensive trowels to avoid the frustration of not being able to find one when needed.

spade

Used for planting and applying mulch. As I never dig the garden in the traditional way, I favour the long handled Devon shovel, known by many names including the Irish potato spade and Cornish shovel. The pointed blade seems to cut into the ground easily, the long handle means there is less bending required.

Left *A few inexpensive tools are all that is required for all but the most extreme pruning jobs.*

Above *Most gardeners will have their favourite piece of kit. Mine is this massive but easy-to-use spade.*

fork

Once the initial garden is set out this is really only needed to turn compost and move manure.

wheelbarrow

Your garden wheels, for moving around plants, mulch, compost, prunings and tools. I have found a large plastic cart on pneumatic tyres a real help as is stable, well engineered, moves smoothly and easily and it has a very large capacity – well worth considering for larger gardens.

watering can

Size matters. You may think it wise to invest in an expensive, outsized watering can but will you want to carry it around the garden when it is full? It pays to choose an attractive, weather-proof can as they often get left around the garden.

twine

There is a plethora of ties available, plastic covered, cushioned, self-fastening and expanding but good old fashioned basic twine looks good, is inexpensive and works well.

secateurs

Used for pruning fruit canes and small growth. A good pair of secateurs is a worthwhile investment. The blades should be kept sharp and in good condition to ensure they cut cleanly. When you buy secateurs they will probably have some indication of the thickness of stem they are designed to cut. If you persistently force them to cut thicker wood they will lose their effectiveness. Use loppers instead.

loppers or long arm pruners

Very useful for reaching higher into trees to prune without having to use a ladder. Loppers will cut thicker growth than secateurs.

pruning saw

A neat little folding saw with teeth designed to cope with pruning.

ladders

In the average garden you are unlikely to want to invest in special fruit picking ladders. If at all possible work from the ground. If you use ladders, ensure they are held in place securely and footed properly.

fruit-picking devices

Another way to avoid using ladders are the various fruit picking devises available. All involve a small basket or cup on a long pole, so the fruit can be dislodged and brought to the ground safely.

Right *If you decide to grow fruit on a large scale, investing in a fruit picking ladder may be a good idea.*

jargon buster

acid
Soils with a pH of under 7 are described as acidic. As the pH becomes lower the soil becomes more acidic. These soils contain no lime and suit blueberries and cranberries.

alkaline
Used to describe soils containing lime with a pH of more than 7. The higher the number becomes the more alkaline the soil. Some plants will not tolerate alkaline soils.

annual
A plant which goes through the cycle of germination to death in one year.

aphid
Small insect including black fly and green fly. They suck sap from plants and congregate on the tender new growth. They excrete a sticky substance called honeydew, which is often feed upon by ants. The main cause for concern is the fact that they spread plant viruses.

bacteria
Single celled organism, can bring about chemical changes in the cells of plants.

ballerina
A single stemmed tree that requires no pruning. Fruit is held close to the single stem and down its entire length.

berry
A fruit containing a number of seeds.

biological control
Using predators and parasites to control pests.

blackfly
See aphid.

bloom
A flower or the fine dusty covering found on plums, grapes and blueberries.

blossom
A mass of flowers on a fruit tree.

branch
The limb of a tree.

break
Removing the growing point of a branch or shoot forces a plant to develop side shoots known as breaks.

brutting
A technique used on hazel trees where shoots are partially broken and left hanging from the tree to restrict growth late in the season.

bud
A small, dormant lump on a branch or stem that may develop into leaves or flowers.

bush
A shrub with no trunk.

calcareous
Chalky.

canker
A fungal and bacterial disease of some fruit trees.

certified stock
Plants guaranteed free from disease.

chlorophyll

Transforms energy from light and gives leaves their green colouration.

clay

A heavy, impervious soil.

codling moth

The maggots commonly found in apples are the larvae of the codling moth.

container plant

A tree or bush which has been grown and is sold in a pot.

cordon

Plants which are trained to grow as a single stem. A double cordon is u-shaped with two stems.

crown

The part of the plant where the stems and roots meet, in strawberries for example. In rhubarb it refers to the whole root system.

defruiting

Removing all the fruitlets from young trees to allow them to use all their energies to establish.

die-back

Shoots wither and die from the growing tip towards the body of the plant. The dead material should be removed.

disease

Attack on the plant by fungi, bacteria or virus.

dormant

Not growing, resting. Most plants lose their leaves during the dormant period. Plants usually become dormant in the coldest part of the year.

drip line

An area around the tree where rain drips from its leaves – this indicates the extent of the trees feeding roots.

drought

A long period without rainfall.

drupe

Peaches, apricots and nectarines are drupes, raspberries and blackberries are compound drupes. The seed of the plant is protected in a hard casing which is, in turn, wrapped in a pulpy layer.

ericaceous

Acidic, lime-free compost for acid-loving plants, or used to describe acid-loving plants like blueberries and cranberries.

espalier

A fruit tree trained to have a central trunk and branches extending horizontally from the trunk on both sides at regular intervals. Normally grown against a wall.

evergreen

Plants which retain their leaves all year round.

fan trained

A method of training fruit trees, normally against a wall, where the tree is grown on a short trunk and branches radiate from the trunk in the manner of a fan.

fire blight

A bacterial disease that affects pears and, to a lesser extent, apples.

foliar spray
To supply a plant with nutrients through the leaves by spraying a liquid feed onto the foliage.

frost resistance
The ability of a plant to withstand varying degrees of cold. Though the plant may survive at a specific temperature, its blossom and fruit may be damaged at low temperatures.

fruit bud
A bud which becomes a flower and then, if pollinated, a fruit.

graft
The shoot inserted into the root stock.

grassing down
Sowing grass under fruit trees, a term used mainly in orchards.

half-standard
A tree with a 1.2 m trunk.

hardening-off
Acclimatising plants to lower outside temperatures when they have been grown under glass or in a protected environment.

heeling-in
Temporarily planting trees or bushes until they can be planted in their permanent spot.

honeydew
A sticky substance excreted by aphids, coating stems and leaves. Ants farm aphids to benefit from the honeydew.

humus
Decomposed organic matter, dark rich brown in colour. It improves water retention and adds nutrients to the soil.

june drop
A normal process in which trees shed a portion of the fruitlets that have formed ensuring the tree can afford to produce the crop it retains. Poor pollination or drought can also cause immature fruit to fall.

leaching
Is a term used to describe nutrients from the soil being removed as they dissolve in rainwater or as plants are watered.

leaf mould
The product of composted leaves, a wonderful soil conditioner.

lime
A form of calcium added to the soil to decrease the acidity. The lime content of the soil will determine its pH.

loam
A fertile, easily worked soil with a perfect balance of clay, sand, silt and humus.

microclimate
Describes a climatic niche in which temperatures and conditions differ from those locally. It is usually applied to a more favourable area on a sheltered terrace or close to a wall.

mulch
Any material used to top dress the soil. It may be organic and add nutrients to the soil or inorganic, like sheet polythene, and merely suppress weeds and protect the surface of the soil.

NPK
The chemical symbols for the main plant foods – nitrogen to encourage leafy growth, phosphorus for root growth and potassium for flowers and fruit.

orchard
An area planted with fruit trees.

organic gardening

Gardening without artificial chemicals.

pest

Any insect or animal which damages a plant but not diseases.

potassium

See NPK.

pruning

Cutting back bushes and trees to improve productivity, remove dead wood or train into a restricted form.

resistant

This refers to plants which have a good chance of warding off an attack of a particular disease. It does not mean immune.

runner

This is a thin stem thrown out by a plant which produces plantlets with roots at the nodes, as with strawberries.

side-shoot

This is the lateral growth growing from the main branches.

stooling

Cutting the entire plant to ground level to encourage new growth.

strig

The term used to describe a cluster of black, red or white currants.

sucker

A shoot coming straight from the roots of a plant. On grafted trees suckers should be removed.

virus

Often transported by aphids, a virus is a sub-microscopic parasitic agent which multiplies in the cells of the plant. Not all viruses are damaging to a plant's growth, but others can attack the plant and possibly kill it.

weed

Any plant growing where it is unwanted by the gardener.

wilt

Foliage droops and withers.

index

Page numbers in *italics* refer to illustrations

Q

R

S

T

V

W

acknowledgements

My thanks to: Clive Nichols for his ravishing photography and endless good humour in the face of long drives, far too early in the morning; David for helping with the endless barrows of manure; David Roberts for skillfully finishing off the woodwork when time was short; Stuart Mansbridge for generously supplying a perfect, photogenic straw bale; my parents for joining me in my enthusiasm for gardening and to my father for sharing with me his vast knowledge of growing blueberries; Emma Pattison and all at New Holland for their hard work; Harriet, Nancy and Joshua for their unfailing interest, honest opinions and once again, putting up with it all.

picture credits

Alamy: pages 59, 73, 89, 121, 129, 130, 134, 140, 141, 143, 144, 148, 151, 162 and 215.